Blessed

to have been

ABANDONED

Published by Mindstir Media, LLC

45 Lafayette Rd | Suite 181| North Hampton, NH 03862 | USA

1.800.767.0531 | www.mindstirmedia.com

Printed in the United States of America

ISBN-13: 978-1-7365224-1-7

Blessed

to have been
ABANDONED

the story of the
Baby Box Lady

written by
Monica Kelsey

MINDSTIR MEDIA

For My Parents

Mom and Dad, thank you for your fierce and unconditional love. I am so grateful that when you were called on June 8, 1973 about a baby girl who needed a home, you responded without hesitation, "Bring me my daughter"!

Adoption Unleashes Possibility!

FOREWORD BY KEVIN HARRINGTON,

ORIGINAL SHARK FROM ABC'S "SHARK TANK"
AND BESTSELLING AUTHOR

As a global entrepreneur, I have the honor to connect with some of the most extraordinary individuals one can imagine. Monica Kelsey stands out as one of those individuals—a resilient and determined woman with a truly special story.

Monica shares her account of being adopted and all the questions, doubts and fears that come along with that. Upon investigation of her biological parents' story, she uncovers a shocking truth about her origins that rattle her to the core. Through Monica's writing, we learn that even the most painful experience can later shift our perspectives and transform into a beautiful catalyst in the future.

Throughout the ups and downs, I've worked hard to recognize some of life's adversities as hidden opportunities. Monica is no stranger to turning adversity into opportunity—not only for personal growth, but to provide inspiration and resources for those most in need.

I believe we have all asked "why me?" during the most pivotal times in our lives, questioning the very purpose of our existence. Monica's story asks and answers that question, as she continues to make a positive impact throughout the nation with her non-profit. As the pioneer of the infomercial business, I know the blood, sweat, and tears that goes into developing a product, let alone one that saves lives. Kudos to Monica for her dedication, faith, and ingenuity! Her work with mothers who are not ready to take on the responsibility of parenthood, with lawmakers on state and national levels, and with the most innocent of all—newborn babies, is a result of seeking and finding her life's purpose.

I had the pleasure of learning Monica's powerful story of turning doubt into action, while enjoying some laughs along the way—truly a lesson for which we can all be grateful.

INTRODUCTION

Love your story and share your testimony, with confidence, because God, Himself, wrote it, and though there are areas and seasons that we wish we could avoid or re-do, the scriptures declare that all things are working together for the good of those who love God (Romans 8:28).

The following pages are my story. The pain, struggle, valleys and mountain tops, all of these pointing to the amazing hand of God. My story, similar to your own, is riddled with questions: "Why"? "Why me"? "Why now", or perhaps "Why not now"? Questioning the providence of God is a part of being human. Asking the tough questions about where He was in the midst of pain and struggle and why He allowed the difficult seasons of our life is common to most of our lives.

If I have learned anything in this amazing adventure called living, it is that God is bigger than my questions, fears and suffering! He can handle your real emotions, and He is ALWAYS there... present, with you. He will never leave you or forsake you. He will never abandon you.

My hope is that by sharing my journey, by inviting you to walk alongside me, that you will be encouraged to see the hand of God in your own journey. If you are just starting out, be encouraged to never give up! If you are in the middle of a valley or a season of suffering, be strong and courageous! If you are approaching the winter of your journey, look back with clear eyes and give thanks for the One who wrote your story and traveled with you the entire way.

You see, it boils down to perspective. If we focus on our circumstances, it will be devastating. But if we keep our **focus on JESUS**, we can walk through whatever life brings. Allow Him to use the darkness for good. He will. Do that and not only will you experience God in ways you would never have otherwise, but you will see Him move and use your journey for His glory. And friends, there is nothing more satisfying than doing what we were created for - bringing glory to Him. Joy, peace, comfort, and rest are found there. So whatever mountain you're facing, keep your eyes on Christ and rest in His grace and grip. There's no safer place to be.

~ *Monica Kelsey*

Chapter 1

MY NAME IS MONICA, AND I AM ADOPTED!

For you created my inmost being;
you knit me together in my mother's womb.
I praise you because I am fearfully and wonderfully made;
your works are wonderful;
I know that full well.

Psalm 139:13-14

I cannot remember a time in my childhood that I was not aware of the fact that I was adopted. Growing up, the concept of "being adopted" was simply normal. There was no great "revelation" of this important event in my history. Growing up in the 70's and 80's, being adopted was often the punchline in sitcoms. When one of the siblings or family members began behaving oddly or getting into trouble, a family member would blurt out "Well, you were adopted", followed by laughter or uncomfortable silence. I never struggled with feeling unloved or unwanted. I had two wonderful parents who cherished me and never once made me feel that I was anything less than their daughter and a precious gift to their family. It would be many years before I would come to understand fully the great gift that my parents were to me.

My parents were married on June 27, 1970 after my dad returned home from the war. Because they had dated for many years, my parents knew they would get married and start a family after he finally returned. As many men do, my dad always prayed for a son, someone who would carry on the family name. Of course, he would have loved and been grateful for any child God graciously provided, but was super excited when on June 2, 1971, he was blessed with a son.

My mom would tell me the story of how my little brother, Robbie, was born two years before me and passed away after only living 24 hours. "He was absolutely beautiful and perfect," mom would say, "all 10 pounds, 8 ounces of him." Mom would always remind us when she would tell Robbie's story: "I know he is in heaven waiting for me and I know he is in good hands." I remember as a child when mom would speak of Robbie, that while she made clear that she trusted God and His reasoning, she never really understood the "why". Today, she would tell you the "why" has become increasingly transparent.

The death of a child is a parent's worst nightmare. As parents we believe that our children will bury us, we certainly do not expect that it will be the parents who bury their child. The loss of a child is one of the most difficult heartbreaks anyone ever faces. For my mom and dad, a parents' worst nightmare became a painful reality on that day in June of 1971. My brother's death was undeniably the worst day of my parents' lives. But through the grief of losing a son, God had a plan to save two little girls.

My older sister was 2-years-old, malnourished and abused. The state stepped in and terminated parental rights and she was placed in the care of my parents. The abuse and neglect suffered by my sister was so severe it almost ended her life, but thank God she was rescued from that abuse and was provided with a forever family.

I was brought to my parents on June 8, 1973 after becoming eligible for adoption. My parents were told that I was placed for adoption because my birth parents were too young to care for me. It would be well into my adulthood before I would learn the entire story.

My older sister and I were chosen by my adoptive parents. My family was then blessed five years later when my mother became pregnant and gave birth to my younger sister. My dad had to quickly adjust to a houseful of GIRLS!

My dad often laughed about having three girls. Living in a huge house with nine rooms and only one bathroom, God obviously had a sense of

---

humor. Today, I think my dad is grateful that his three girls are married with families of their own because he can now take hot showers instead of the ice cold showers he took in the past. I distinctly remember on many occasions we would hear coming from the bathroom: "Who used all the hot water?" I, of course, would be the first to respond, "Not me; it was your other daughters!" My younger sister, always the "informer", would respond right back that it was me who had been in the bathroom for over an hour. In my defense, it takes a bit of time to look this good!

Being a "middle" child came with its challenges. When we were young, my older sister used to hook me up to a dog chain and make me drink from a dog bowl. I think she thought this was a "fun" game. When she started making me eat dog treats, it finally dawned on me that I was getting the raw end of this deal! Although the dog treats weren't bad, they kind of tasted like bacon, I had to finally put a stop to this bit of playtime fun. My older sister had a reputation for being bossy, typical "eldest child" syndrome, and I was known as "the instigator". My younger sister was forever "the informer". This was precisely the reason she was sent with me in my teen years to most parties. She would inevitably fill my parents in immediately upon our return. I am sure you can deduce my parents' reasoning for sending the informer with the instigator. For some reason it never worked out well for me and I was constantly grounded.

I had a very special relationship with my dad. I truly am a "daddy's girl".

As I drive the rural roads to my childhood home today on a trip to visit my dad who is battling cancer, I pass the high school softball field. So many beautiful memories of my dad, who coached our summer league team and spent countless hours on that field patiently coaching me personally. He was my biggest fan and encourager then, and remains the same today. As painful as it is to watch the suffering and pain as he bravely battles this horrible disease, I am so grateful for this man that was a gift from God to me. My deep appreciation for the love of my heavenly father, comes from an earthly father who was a powerful testament to unconditional, unfailing love. He remains my first true love.

Growing up an adoptee has come with a host of emotions that many fail to understand. Some people believe that happy adoptees, and those adopted as infants, have no hurt feelings of loss or abandonment. But the truth is that ALL adoption involves loss, and then requires grieving. This grieving looks differently for every adoptee.

Adoption is wonderful and adoption has the potential to positively change many lives. It is wrong to assume that adoptees who were adopted as infants do not grieve the loss of their birth family and birth identity. Adoption is confusing. A part of me would be forever thankful adoption was a big part of my reality and my childhood. Another part of me was stuck in the unknown and confusion that is adoption – wondering about all the 'what if's' in life.

My parents were always open and honest with me, giving me the information they were told when they adopted me. They shared that my biological parents were in love, young and couldn't care for me so they did what they felt was best and placed me for adoption. This information always made me imagine I had a fairy tale family waiting for me with open arms, and that when I got old enough to meet them, we would run into each other's arms and ride off into the sunset. I used this little fantasy to my advantage more than once, especially as a teen. I remember specific occasions when mom and dad and I would be engaged in an argument, I would lash out at them and tell them that I hated them and petulantly inform them of the fact that even though they didn't love me, my "real" (envision the finger air quotes) Mom loved me and one day I would find her. I vividly remember my mom consistently responding; "We know you're upset right now, so we will love you enough for the both of us until you're no longer angry". This statement always made me angrier but I would eventually manage to get over it, as two parents stubbornly chose to love unconditionally.

As many adoptees experience, one of my deeper inner struggles was that I didn't look like my parents. I longed to look like them and when someone would make the comment that I looked just like my mom, I would smile but I knew the truth. I used to dream about sitting around a table with all my biological family and seeing all the traits in them that I carry myself. I remember seeing other families who bore that family resemblance and wishing that I knew who it was that I resembled. Did I have any biological siblings and did anyone out there look like me.

The most common occasion in which the "what if" questions would come into my consciousness were those times I would inevitably be asked, "Do you want to find your birth family?" While well meaning, the inquisitor most likely did not realize they had just asked a difficult and very personal question.

This is an extremely loaded question and it still surprises me that this was often one of the first questions I would be asked growing up. I often felt the pressure to just say a simple yes or no, but it is definitely not that simple. The person who would ask that question is completely unaware of my origin story or that at that time, I was completely unaware of the true circumstances surrounding my conception and adoption. It is also a difficult question to answer because while I loved and cared for my birth family, and would often fantasize about who they were and what their story was, I didn't have a crystal ball and could never portend to know the future. I couldn't possibly anticipate what would happen if somehow, I met these people who were at that time complete strangers to me. Would it be good to meet? Bad? Would they agree to meet me? Had they told anyone in their lives about me? There are so many things that would have to happen in order to find them, and just thinking about that was emotional. This question would inevitably cause me to think about what they look like, what are they doing with their lives? I wondered if they were okay or were they grieving the loss that I was grieving; asking the questions about me that I was certainly asking myself about them?

This then, is what drove me to become an "expert" private investigator and as a teen and young adult, I went to great lengths with limited resources, to unravel the mystery that was my beginning. We didn't have "google" or "Ancestory.com". Heck, we didn't have the internet! So I had to do my research the slow and tedious way.

Through my expert investigation I was able to discover my birth mother's identity. Because I was in my early twenties, and after learning some of the struggles in her life at that time, I worried that neither one of us was in a place to build a relationship, and any attempt to do so would not have a good outcome. I decided to put this information and knowledge of my birth mom on the back burner for a time, and allow a few years to pass and life experience to accumulate.

After graduating High School, I enlisted in the United States Navy. I spent the next eight years serving and defending my country. I was honorably discharged and then met the love of my life, Joe, married and started a family.

It would be years and three beautiful children later, that the meeting I had fantasized about for so long would finally take place.

Chapter 2

SANDY'S STORY

"But he said to me, "My grace is sufficient for you, for my power is made perfect in weakness." Therefore I will boast all the more gladly about my weaknesses, so that Christ's power may rest on me." -2 Corinthians 12:9

There are moments in our lives that define us--that push us, sometimes kicking and screaming, to become the person we were designed to be from the beginning, by the One who "formed us in our mother's womb". For some, it's a series of life events, but for others, it's a single, defining moment of clarity that hits you like a bolt of lightning from the heavens. For me, this single, defining moment was meeting my birth mother and discovering that I was a child conceived, not in love, but by a brutal act of violence.

At the age of 37, I reconnected with my birth-mother. The day I reconnected with her I drove to the state of Michigan to reunite with her. My heart was racing as I walked up to her front door with my husband by my side and knocked three knocks. She answered the door and I was in awe of her. She was all of 4'11", blond hair, blue eyes and 100 pounds soaking wet. I didn't look a thing like her. She invited us in and I couldn't take my eyes off her. I am sure she was feeling like I was staring at her but I just wanted to see every characteristic that she had to see if this was something I possess also. The first thing I noticed was that she speaks with her hands. This is something that I have done my whole life. Her hands also looked just like mine, or mine looked like hers if you want to get technical. She also has a chin like a "butt" and unfortunately I received this trait also. But these two traits were really all I saw of myself in her.

This was painful for me because I still held on to that childhood dream. I always hoped that when I found my birth mother, we would look exactly alike, that I would see myself when I looked at her. She was absolutely beautiful in every way, but I only had a few of her features or characteristics. As I sat there in her living room holding my husband's hand, the inevitable question came up. It was the proverbial elephant in the room that had to be addressed: "Who was my birth-father"? I was completely unprepared to hear the story that was about to be dropped like a bomb in my world.

Sandy immediately got up from her chair and walked back to her bedroom and returned with a blue folder that was tattered and worn. She pulled out a police report. Sandy began to tell me the story of a dark night in 1972. She was just 17 years old doing what teenagers have done for generations, partying with friends while parents think you are studying. On this night, she accepted a ride home from a person who she did not personally know, completely oblivious to the danger. This man didn't take her home, but rather took her to a dark road a few miles outside of town and violently beat and raped her. After he finished his attack, he left her on the side of the road to die or at the very least to find her own way home. Bloodied and traumatized physically and emotionally, she walked all the way home, went straight to her room and sobbed alone on her bed. This night marked the beginning of decades of pain and desolation for young Sandy!

The next morning Sandy confided in her mother. The story came out in waves of pain. Her mother urgently took her to the hospital and then to the police station. As Sandy relayed this awful story to me; I naively, and rather selfishly, kept wondering what this all had to do with me? I certainly felt awful for her and my heart broke listening to her share this life shattering experience, but I still had no idea why she was telling me all these horrific details about her past.

Sandy continued this gruesome tale. She explained that just when she had finally begun to feel like her life was getting back to some semblance of normal, she discovered the unthinkable; she was pregnant. She was devastated. Her mind raced, what will people say? Will she be known as the town slut for a crime she didn't commit? She told me that this was the exact moment she fell into a complete depression. Sandy said that she cried for weeks.

Completely wrecked, the 17 year old gathered all the courage she could muster and confided in her mother. Her mother was equally devastated, angry and shocked.

Finally, with advice from her mother, she began to contemplate the option of an illegal abortion. She explained to me that she wanted to "get her life back!" In her mind, if she could make this new life go away, then she could go on with her life like nothing ever happened. She tried to convince herself that having an illegal abortion would put her life back together again. But the truth remains, no amount of cash, or drugs, surgical instruments or for that matter, all the king's horses and all the king's men, would ever be able to put things back together again.

Sandy's perception of her mothers' feelings at the time was that she was extremely angry. This was 1972 and having an unwed, pregnant daughter, no matter what the circumstances, would surely ruin the families' reputation. In no uncertain terms, her mother communicated that this baby was an unwelcome and unwanted complication to an already horrible chapter in her short existence.

The day of the procedure arrived, and Sandy's mother drove her frightened, damaged, distraught 17- year old daughter to the back alley abortionist. But with extraordinary courage and determination, as Sandy stood in front of the man who was about to snuff out the life of her tiny baby; Sandy changed her mind. She walked right out of that dark, seedy place that smelled of death and never looked back.

A victim of an era where unwed mothers were hidden from the world, Sandy's mom did just that and hid her at home, keeping her locked away from everyone. Even when Sandy's own father passed away, she was not allowed to attend the funeral for fear that someone would know her daughter was pregnant.! She was completely isolated and alone.

It was some six months later, and two hours after giving birth to a baby girl in Ohio, Sandy and her mother left this newborn at a hospital in April of 1973. Suddenly, as Sandy recounted this horrifically painful story, a lightbulb went on in my brain, and like a bolt of lightning ripping into my consciousness, it became clear! Sandy was sharing not only HER story, but MY story! I was that newborn baby girl. I was the child she left.

In that moment, all of my childhood fantasies of a young mother and father, who simply couldn't afford to be parents and wanted the best for their baby and lovingly made an "adoption plan", were completely shattered. I was conceived in rape, my biological father is a rapist.

I began to put the pieces together because I was born in April of 1973. I don't think that it fully hit me until my husband and I were sitting in our Jeep in her driveway getting ready to leave. Before Joe started the vehicle, he sat in the driver's seat staring at me. I looked back at him and he said "Are you ok"? In my mind I was wondering why he was asking me this and without hesitation I said "yes". The drive home was silent, I was still processing all she had said. The next few weeks were equally as silent. I became more and more distant and angry. I couldn't understand how this could be my life. My exact words at the time were "this sucks, I don't want this to be my life"!

There are few discoveries about your past that can shatter like this one. All of the deep questions came rushing into my psyche, "Did God 'plan' me or was I some horrible accident?" "Would I have been better off aborted?" "Was I simply 'the rapists' baby' 'Spawn of Satan' 'Demon Seed' or any of those other horrible names I had heard uttered by those justifying an abortion?" You see, all of these labels have been used for children like me, sometimes by those who call themselves "pastor" or "bishop". I had heard the simple justification for the murder of babies conceived from rape on countless occasions by those who claimed to stand for life, "I am against abortion, except in the case of rape". Truth be told, it was a justification I had once held myself primarily because it was never about ME. Funny how our perspective changes drastically when a political talking point becomes poignantly personal.

As the days became weeks and the weeks became months, I began to look at my life as a lie. Instead of being the loved and cherished daughter of my adoptive parents, I was an unwanted child thrust into this world by violence. I questioned my life, my very existence, in a world that once held so much meaning. Was I alive by a mere stroke of luck, or by the grace of God? Was I merely an unloved and unwanted baby thrust into the arms of parents looking for the "perfect" child? There are seminal moments in everyone's life when who and what they thought they were is challenged in a deeply profound and earth-shattering way. I began to look at my life from a distance, as if through a telescope, with only a pinprick of light visible at the very end. How was I supposed to pick myself up and continue to live a life now deemed as a mistake from the start? How could I go on pretending I didn't know the truth? Was this punishment? Why did God choose this life for me?

I felt very angry with God. I became very bitter and even started to question my faith. I became depressed and was drowning in self pity. I remember telling myself out loud, over and over again, "this really sucks". Was this punishment for some of the crazy things I did when I was younger, some sort of sick karma? Why me? Why ME?

Finally, I decided to reach out to a friend who found help for me as I struggled with these issues. Telling this friend had its own challenges. As the truth about my very beginning became increasingly public, how was I going to justify my existence to the world?

I struggled for months, but eventually, with support from the right people and a mentor that showed me how my testimony and Sandy's story could not only help me, but may help others, I began to entertain the idea that perhaps I could tell her story publicly. So I decided to give it a try.

I spoke for the first time at Butler University in Indianapolis. I have to tell you, it was almost like therapy for me to tell it. Publically telling my story and Sandy's, gradually grew into a process of healing, emotionally and spiritually. The more I walked on a stage and shared my pain and struggle, the more aware I became of just how important my words were to a culture that desperately needed a voice for the "least of these".

The deeply personal struggle of coming to peace with your beginnings, of asking God the hard questions, sometimes in a fit of tears, cannot be limited to a few paragraphs on paper. The theological question about why God allows "bad things" to happen to "good" people will echo in human minds until He comes again and all tears are wiped away. It will be then, and only then that we will "see clearly" what we now view through this earthly veil. But let me tell you what I do see clearly; your life matters. You matter to God and He sees you and knows you. His plan for you is good, plans not to harm you, but to give you a future and hope. This is true for you and it is true for me. And it is true for every child conceived, wanted or unwanted by human parents; with wine and roses or through violence. My life matters to the Creator, my life has eternal value to HIM. He formed ME in my mother's womb, and wept with her through the pain and still holds me in His arms as I struggle to find meaning in all of this pain . My all powerful God is in the business of making all things new. "And we know that in all things God works for the good of those who love him, who have been called according to his purpose." Romans 8:28 NIV

I often wonder what my life would be like had I never spent those years searching for Sandy and never uncovered the truth of my conception and birth. Would I still be attending church "some" Sundays and carving out exceptions for abortion if the child was conceived in rape? Maybe so, but thankfully, with all of its struggle, I am so glad I pursued her and the truth. You see, having met and spent time with my birth mother, my life has been radically changed. I have become a more thoughtful and empathetic person, a more grateful daughter, and a stronger follower of Christ.

As time went by, I continued to ask all of the hard questions and struggle with the truth, all the while continuing to speak publicly about my past. I know that part of the healing process is to speak up, to be a voice for the most vulnerable who are being" led to slaughter". I could, and must be a part of the movement to rescue these innocents. Little did I know that one more "bombshell" revelation involving my first hours of life would once again shake my world and propel me into one more gigantic mission.

Chapter 3

FROM MY FIRST BREATH TO HER LAST

"I will not cause pain without allowing something new to be born" Isaiah 66:9"

On a spring day in March of 2013, I received a call that my birth mother was in the hospital in Michigan and not doing well. At the age of 57, she had contracted a urinary tract infection that went septic. For those not in the medical field, an infection that gets into the bloodstream can be fatal. For seven days, she was on a ventilator fighting for her life, and for seven days, I was sitting beside her, praying that God would give me more time with the woman who had sacrificed so much to bring me into this world. Those seven days became some of the hardest days of my life to talk about.

While spending days at the hospital by Sandy's bedside, I had the opportunity to meet my birth cousin. Teresa was the daughter of Sandy's brother. Sandy was the youngest of 4 and the only girl in the family. Teresa was just a few years older than me. She had come to the hospital to see Sandy as her condition was worsening. Teresa and Sandy were very close as Teresa spent many weekends and summer days staying with Sandy on her small farm with chickens and goats. Teresa remembers being aware of the" family secret", the fact that Sandy had gotten pregnant as a teen and had placed a child for adoption in the early 70's, but the rumor was that it was a baby boy. She knew better than to have asked Sandy directly the details about said "family secret" .

Teresa was and I were in a small waiting room outside of Sandy's hospital room, as only a small number of visitors were allowed by her side at one time. I introduced myself to Teresa as Sandy's biological daughter. That was a bombshell. Not only that I existed, but I was a girl! As Teresa and I talked about my adoption and the family secret that was now a living and breathing woman sitting in front of her, I asked a simple "get to know you" question. "What do you do for work?" Teresa replied, "I'm a firefighter/medic". Again, my jaw hit the floor! I believe my verbal response was "Shut the front door!" When I told her that I, too, was a firefighter/medic, we were both in shock. What are the chances! Female firefighter/medics are not as common as you would think, and here was my biological cousin, whom I had just met, in the exact same career as myself. This was a real foreshadowing and example of God's hand as He prepared me for the mission ahead.

On the 4th day of her hospitalization, the doctors reported improvements in Sandy's test results. My husband and I were encouraged, and we decided to head home and see our children. Joe and I had been at the hospital every day, and finally on this night we felt she was strong enough for us to go home and spend a bit of time with our kids. We lived three hours away from the hospital and we were completely exhausted as we had been keeping round the clock vigil at her side. Sandy was still on a ventilator and couldn't talk. Before we left, I kissed her cheek and said, "Love ya girlfriend, you are my hero". A single tear trickled down her cheek.

Arriving at the hospital the next morning, I was met with the distressing news that she had slipped into a coma during the night. At the time I had kissed her cheek and whispered in her ear the night before, I didn't realize those words would be the last I spoke to her or I certainly would have said so much more.

Sandy fought for three more days, but on day seven, the doctor delivered the devastating news: She was dying, and nothing more could be done. My heart sank and all the hopes and dreams of a future with the woman who had given me life sank, too. That day I sat for hours watching the monitor and tracking every beat of her heart, every breath she took. Eventually, her heart beats slowed as did her breathing. My eyes were glued to the monitor. I was terrified that if I looked away, even for a second, the monitor would go silent and dark. The slower the beat of her heart, the more I fell apart. Then she took one last breath and her heart stopped. As I held my birth mother's hand in those final moments, my husband held me. I could feel his arms tighten around my waist--his presence an anchor gifted by God during one of life's stormy moments.

Although I tried to be strong for Sandy's husband, I completely fell apart! Tears flowed as I stood in incredulously thinking about what my life would be without her presence, her courage, and her strength. This woman who had fought so hard for my life, carrying me to term, all the while knowing she couldn't provide for me all of the things I needed to survive, knowing that I needed a mother and a father, lovingly gave my Mom and Dad, the most precious of gifts, a baby daughter. The most selfless gift a mother can give is her child, and she gave me freely, with no reservations. How blessed I am to have been given a gift of such magnitude, one that can never be repaid. She believed in me until the day she died, and I believed in her. She was with me when I took my first breath, and I was holding her hand when she took her last. I am continually amazed by God's plan and purpose. He allowed Sandy to be there for me when I needed her the most and what amazing grace that He allowed me to be there for her when she needed me the most!

After Sandy's passing, I continued speaking about both of our journey's and celebrated this "hero" in my life who had suffered so much in order to bring me safely into the world. The Fall just prior to Sandy's home going, I went to Indianapolis to speak on behalf of then Candidate for Senate, Richard Mourdock, who was being crucified in the media for a statement about rape conception in a debate. Mourdock responded when asked about abortion in the case of rape or incest: "I think even when life begins in that horrible situation of rape, that's something God intended to happen." Of course this immediately was misconstrued as him stating that "God planned the rape". Mourdock explained after the debate he did not believe God intended the rape, but that God is the only one who can create life. Every life, regardless of circumstance of conception, had a plan and purpose by God.

Myself, and many others who were conceived in rape, or who became pregnant as a result of rape, met together to record our testimonies in support of Richard Mourdock. At that taping, I met a woman by the name of Pam Stenzel, who would become an integral part of my story moving forward.

25

Pam Stenzel was also conceived in rape, adopted and loved. She has spent her adult life working with women in crisis pregnancies through life affirming pregnancy help centers. She also began speaking to young people about sexual integrity and choosing to save sex for marriage, thus avoiding many painful outcomes. At this time she was speaking to approximately 500,000 students in school assemblies, youth conferences and churches every year. Pam and I immediately bonded, some people still say we look like sisters, me being the much younger sister, of course! Because I really wanted to expand my outreach and get more experience with public speaking, I asked Pam to help me work on my skills as a speaker.

I never gave up my detective work as to my origins and the circumstances around my conception and birth and subsequent adoption. Being the timid and non confrontational person that I am, I boldly tracked down my biological father. Something in me just needed to understand that half of my gene pool, and I felt some sense of justice for Sandy in confronting him with my existence. My very patient husband accompanied me to the address where bio dad resided. We continued to drive by his house for hours, before I decided to stop and walk up to the front door and introduce myself. Needless to say, this did not go well. With some choice words that I will not repeat here, his wife in no uncertain terms told me to take a flying leap.

Further delving into the details of my adoption, I began to ask some pretty pointed questions of my adoptive parents. I wanted to see the paperwork, my adoption records, original birth certificate and other evidence of those first few days of life before I was placed in the arms of my adoptive family. Continuing to investigate all of these details had nothing to do with not feeling welcomed, accepted or loved by my adoptive parents. In fact, nothing could be further from the truth. As an example, my mother, who did such a thorough job of treating all of us girls exactly the same, never pointing out the biological difference, gave my sister and I a great laugh one day.

My mom called me on the phone and evidently, she had just discovered "The Maury Show". She proceeds to inform me that she is going to "take my dad on there to do a paternity test on Gina and I." I responded, " Mom, we were adopted!" She replied, "I know that, but it would be funny to hear Maury say that he is not the father and I am not the mother!" Oh my goodness, I could only respond, "Mom! Have you checked your sugar lately cause I think it's low"! She then proceeded to contact my other sister, Gina, who was also adopted and told her the same thing. Gina had the same response "Mom, have you checked your sugar today?"

This continued detective work on my part unveiled another huge blow to my understanding of my identity and beginning. While searching for the adoption paperwork, it finally became clear that Sandy had not "placed me for adoption". She never legally relinquished her parental rights, she simply abandoned me at the hospital and walked away. Of course, now having an understanding of all she had been through, and the added shame of one parent hiding her from everyone in the world, and the horrible loss of the other parent who had passed away in the middle of the biggest crisis in her young life, I fully empathize with the "why". But that empathy does not necessarily soften the blow! I was not lovingly placed for adoption, I was abandoned. I was left in the hands of the state of Ohio to decide my future and fate.

This was a lot to take in! I have now learned that not only was I conceived in rape but I was also abandoned at birth! I immediately had this strong feeling that I had lost an incredible amount of "worth" as a human being. It was as if my life wasn't worth living simply because I was conceived in rape, and then discarded like so much refuse. As a medic/firefighter I had always felt so much personal satisfaction working on the ambulance and I would be overwhelmed with thankfulness everytime I would save someone's life. It is a rush that most people wouldn't understand but every medic/firefighter feels. There is this amazing sense of accomplishment you have when someone's life is hanging in the balance and you are the one standing between life and death for this patient. Then, when you receive the gratitude and praise from the patient and their family, for just doing your job, it is an instant satisfaction. On the other hand, I also lost some people that I couldn't save. There were times when I was working a code, that I worked much longer and harder than I probably should have. Everytime I lost someone, it sent me back a few steps.

I remember very vividly a night when we were called to a house fire at two am in the morning. The only information we were given was that there were no adults in the home, but there were seven kids. As we arrived on scene there were two sheets draped over the bodies of two of the children in the front yard. I immediately grabbed one of the kids that the firefighters were carrying out of the house who wasn't breathing and didn't have a heartbeat. I frantically started working on her and we got a pulse back and transported her to the closest hospital. I immediately felt that satisfaction of saving a life, not that any other medic wouldn't have done the same thing, but it wasn't any other medic, it was me. The next day, this young girl passed away. Her injuries were too much for her little body to take. As painful as her death was, I realized that my efforts had given this young girl's parents twenty four hours to say goodbye to their daughter. These last precious 24 hours would not have been possible if we hadn't worked so hard to save her in the grass outside that burning house. I had the honor to attend her funeral, and at the service I was able to tell the parents that I was the medic that took care of their daughter that night, and they expressed their deep gratitude for my efforts and shared how much it meant to them. This again, fed my deep need to feel "worthy", that ghost of "you matter" I was constantly chasing.

I remember calling my friend Pam, from my driveway, and pouring out my heart, my confusion and my pain. How do I deal with this new revelation, how do I assimilate yet another kernel of the truth into my psyche? How do I stop chasing this illusive ghost of needing to "matter", to make sense of my very existence. Knowing I was trying so hard to find purpose in the pain, Pam began to share with me the "Safe Haven Law" that was available in different forms in the United States. She explained that while working in the pregnancy help centers, they would make sure young women were aware of this option. She further shared that she had never known a mother who had chosen this option, and reminded me that the law was probably not even around in 1973, but she encouraged me to do some research. Being a firefighter/medic I knew there was a safe haven law but I couldn't tell you what it really was. No one had ever come and trained any of us or even talked about it. The extent of my knowledge was that if I was on shift and someone dropped off a baby, I should call my supervisor and they would handle it. Certainly more needed to be done to educate our community and our first responders about the Safe Haven Laws and to protect newborns from illegal abandonment. Is it possible that this important work was what God was preparing me to do. Maybe, just maybe, telling this part of my story in my speaking ministry would help bring awareness to this important option for women in crisis.

Pam was scheduled to do a speaking tour for two weeks at the end of that year in the country of South Africa. She invited me to join her for that trip, and to share my testimony and story of hope in Johannesburg and Cape Town. I knew this was an incredible opportunity to learn, and to make a real difference in the lives of others. I excitedly accepted and that December, Pam and I boarded a flight from Atlanta to Johannesburg, not fully understanding what was about to be birthed in me.

Chapter 4

THE BIRTH OF A DREAM (VISION)

"Every experience God gives us, every person He puts into our lives, is the perfect preparation for a future only He can see." Corrie ten Boom

As I packed my suitcase, and prepared to fly to Johannesburg, South Africa, I had no idea just how this trip would drastically change my life. I was struggling with so many conflicting emotions. Excitement and anticipation for the journey ahead were probably the strongest, but that feeling of worthlessness and despair was constantly nagging at me. I was thrilled to have the opportunity to share my story, and Sandy's story. I had already witnessed how powerfully this story impacted others, but somewhere in quiet moments, the voice of the enemy saying "You were unwanted, unloved, a mistake, abandoned like garbage" continued to whisper in my ear. At times, we can choose to speak truth to the lies the enemy persists in perpetuating. At other times, it takes a profound experience for the voice of truth to come crashing in. I was about to have just that experience.

Pam and I met at the Atlanta airport and had a direct flight from Atlanta to Johannesburg. We had the opportunity, because it was a long flight, to talk about the few weeks in front of us, the different events at which we would be presenting and what we were hoping to accomplish. I was excited about the variety of audiences we would be addressing. From schools, to youth events, Church groups, maternity homes and meeting with those on the frontlines of the prolife movement in Johannesburg. It was going to be action packed, and a great opportunity for me to speak in a variety of settings. I was really looking forward to how it would stretch me as a communicator.

We landed in Johannesburg on December 4th, 2013 and before we could even acclimate to the time zone change, South Africa was rocked by the death of Nelson Mandela. It was surreal to be in Johannesburg and experience first hand the 10 days of national mourning as heads of state descended on the country from all over the world.

It was such a special experience to actually be in South Africa during this time and to learn more about the life and mission of this amazing world figure. Nelson Mandella made an incredible impact not only on his home country, but around the world as he spent his life fighting aparthed and bringing democracy and racial equality to South Africa. He suffered imprisonment for a cause he was willing to die for and later in the trip when we were on top of Table Top mountain in Capetown, we would look down on Robben Island Prison where he spent 18 of the 27 years of his imprisonment. He was awarded the Nobel Peace Prize for his work in dismantling aparthied in South Africa.

As I listened to stories of his passion, his commitment to social justice and racial equality, two quotes specifically stood out and made a dramatic impact on me that week:

*"I learned that courage was not the absence of fear,
but the triumph over it…. The brave man is not he who does not feel afraid,
but he who conquers that fear."*

*"Everyone can rise above their circumstances and achieve success if they are
dedicated to and passionate about what they do."*

I will never forget that Sunday, December 8, attending mass at St. Peter Claver Catholic Church in Soweto, listening to the singing and watching these precious people celebrate the life of their beloved hero. You did not have to understand the language to feel the deep love they had for Nelson Mandella and the deep gratitude for all he had spent his life sacrificing and fighting for. He inspired not only a nation, but the whole world.

With this solemn remembrance occupying the background, we began our speaking tour. The week was filled with so much hope and joy. It seemed that even though we were talking about difficult topics; sex, choices, abortion and abandonment; the message of hope and purpose kept shining through. Not just in the sharing of my story, but in the responses of those who came to hear and learn. At the last minute, I decided to pack my fire gear, to use as a strong visual of my occupation as a firefighter/medic. I would bring the testimony full circle as I explained that although the beginning of my existence was filled with pain and abandonment, this abandoned child was now rescuing and saving the lives of others. I reminded them that not only was I willing to run into a burning building to save lives, I would never discriminate on whose life I was saving and I would always go back in, even for just one! Every life has value, irrespective of skin color, gender, disability or "wantedness".

After an amazing week in Johannesburg that impacted me personally, as much as my story impacted those who listened, we boarded a plane to Cape Town, completely unaware of the bigger impact on my life that was about to take place.

From flat-topped Table Mountain down to the blue waters of Table Bay, Cape Town is simply stunning. We had the opportunity, between events, to pet a cheetah, and to sit on top of Table Mountain and look down on Robben Island Prison. We visited the Cape of Good Hope, where the Atlantic and Indian Oceans meet and you can meet some penguins up close. We met friends who own a beautiful winery on the mountainside, where we sipped wine and talked about the pro life efforts in that part of Africa.

One afternoon, after visiting with moms and moms to be, at a maternity home and having the fun of cuddling newborns, we drove past about 5 paragliders jumping off the mountain. Of course, the instigator herself, informed Norman, our driver and film producer, that I wanted to do that! Norman pulled over and I inquired about the cost. It was only $100 US to jump off the mountain tandem. I couldn't wait! Of course, Pam wanted no part of this crazy adventure and thought I was completely out of my mind to jump off a mountain with a complete stranger, basically attached to a glorified kite! Norman and Pam agreed to take pictures and video of the crazy American firefighter who had no fear for her own safety.

Cameras rolling, My "professional" paragliding pilot, who was about 6'4" strapped me in and gave instructions on how the take-off was going to happen. Pam thought it was quite fun to take a picture of me in a very "compromised" position as I was bent over in front of the instructor while he explained the take off process. We had a great laugh sending that particular photo to my husband Joe!

I should mention here that I am all of 5'1' on a good day, and as my tandem partner began running with me in front, yelling for me to run in unison, all Pam and Norman could see were my little legs moving like crazy, running through the air, touching absolutely nothing! We crashed on first take off and all I could hear was Pam's laughter! On take off number 2, (which was much less dramatic) we sailed off the mountain, it was so exhilarating. I looked down over the city and the bay as we glided through the air. There was a "gopro" camera attached to the helmet of the pilot, so I have the entire ride on video. A few minutes in, it occurs to me to ask the man, "where are we landing"? And maybe more importantly," how am I getting back to my friends I left back on the mountain"? Who just jumps off a mountain without any thought to where you would end up? Back at the top, Pam is asking the same question. She suddenly realized they had watched people jump off the mountain and didn't see anyone return. What were we thinking!

We landed near the ocean, and I proceeded to get into a small van with all of the other paragliders and pilots. I was the only woman and the smallest person in the cramped van so I had the privilege of riding on a lap the whole trip back up the mountain. But I did it and I survived! It was simply amazing! And well, I would do it again if I ever have the chance.

On one of the last nights in Cape Town, Pam and I were scheduled to speak to teens and parents at King of Kings Church in partnership with Living Hope, a huge and extensive ministry born out of this church that seeks to reach people for Christ, bringing hope and breaking the despair of poverty and disease. In 2007, Living Hope was recognized for the Courageous Leadership Award, awarded by the Willow Creek Association and World Vision, to honour a local church that is making a mark in history to battle against HIV and AIDS.

Living Hope from its outset dreamed of exactly what it is today. The work of Healthcare, Substance Abuse Recovery, Life Skills and Agricultural training continues – all going forward seeking to do God's work in God's way. It was truly an amazing experience to visit this outreach in it's many capacities and see first hand the impact on the lives of so many people in Cape Town.

As we were walking into the church, we noticed what appeared to be a "bank deposit" looking contraption with a sign above that read "Hope 4 Babies" and instructions on using the metal "box" below that had the words "www.babysafe.org" etched on the top and many small heart-shaped holes covering the front door. I immediately turned to our host and asked "What is that?"

She explained that over the years there had been infants abandoned and left to die near the church. The last incident, prior to installing the "baby safe", happened while young boys from the church were playing soccer on the church property and spotted a duffle bag that appeared to be moving. They went over to inspect it, and inside found a newborn baby boy, umbilical cord still attached, crying desperately. They immediately notified adults and called for emergency help. Thankfully the little boy survived and was adopted by a family who attended the church. They named him "Moses". At the time we saw the baby safe, little Moses was 7 years old. After discovering baby Moses, the pastor was determined that not another infant would be abandoned on their property and made the decision to install this device to provide a safe and anonymous option for surrendering a newborn.

I was stunned! I had never heard of such a thing and was pretty sure that they didn't exist back home. It was as if lightning struck the ground in front of me. I took pictures of the box, asked every question I could think to ask about the baby safe. I was completely distracted while Pam was speaking, my mind could only think of that safe built in the wall, and baby Moses and the other babies who were spared because their mothers had a safe option to anonymously surrender their newborn.

Sitting on my flight back to the United States, I wrote down my thoughts, plans and dreams for a safe haven baby box to be available in my hometown, and specifically at my fire station in Woodburn, Indiana. There on that Delta napkin, I also sketched my vision of what a "baby box" in America would look like since baby boxes didn't exist in America yet. As I continued to stare at the scribbled notes and drawing, the vision of putting these "baby boxes" in America for the first time, became exciting. It felt a little like I was about to jump off a mountain, having no idea where I would land.

Chapter 5

THE STATE OF INFANT ABANDONMENT AND THE SAFE HAVEN LAWS IN THE UNITED STATES

Many are the plans in a person's heart,
but it is the Lord's purpose that prevails.

Proverbs 19:21

As soon as I arrived back home in Indiana I began my research. I dove straight into the news articles about abandonments across the United States, as well as the existing safe haven laws and how they were being utilized and enforced. The stories broke my heart in pieces.

Late one evening, a young teen in Daphne, Alabama, whose quavering voice on a minutelong tape tells the local police dispatcher she has just left her newborn under a bush near an apartment complex.

"I'm 15 years old and just had a baby," she whimpers to the police dispatcher.

"Would you like to talk to a counselor?"

"My mom's gonna get me," sobbed the girl who called herself "Julie" shortly before hanging up. She feared what repercussions might come when her family inevitably would learn the baby's father was not white.

By the time Daphne police located the shopping bag and carefully

MONICA KELSEY

unwrapped the towel to find insects crawling about the tiny girl's lifeless face, it was too late.

Most of the information I found on the Safe Haven Laws credits Texas with the first law, passed in 1999, to protect infants from abandonment. However, it was the above incident and 2 others where infants were found in a toilet and in bushes outside an apartment, that spurred the city of Mobile, Alabama to create an ordinance they dubbed "Secret Safe Place for Newborns" in 1998. Not only did local NBC reporter, Jodi Brooks, believe something had to be done, she knew that changing the law would not bring about change without awareness. She was determined that these stories, and the new provision for mothers in crisis to leave a newborn with medical staff with no fear of prosecution, would be told and told often.

The first newborn saved as a result of the program was a baby boy, born on Christmas Eve in 1998. The staff at Springhill Medical Center named him Nick after St. Nick. Little Nick got so much attention, his story appeared on Oprah Winfrey.

That same fall, there was this story out of Minnesota:

Early one morning in November of 1998, three men in Red Wing, Minnesota, went fishing for walleye in the Mississippi River. Instead, they found the body of a newborn girl-umbilical cord still attached-floating in the icy waters. Fifty miles north of Red Wing. Parishioners at the Cathedral of St. Paul vowed never to let that happen again. Led by their parish priest, Rev. Andrew Cozzens, they persuaded local hospitals to allow women to anonymously drop off their newborns, no questions asked.

I was noticing that in these early stories, communities and concerned individuals were taking it upon themselves to do something, even if their state laws did not provide for the intervention. In fact in the Pittsburgh region, after about a dozen babies had been abandoned, Gigi Kelly, mother of 3 was prompted to start a "Basket for Babies" program. Over 600 families participated and placed baskets filled with blankets on their front porches with their porch lights turned on.

These early stories, along with 13 infants abandoned in the Houston, Texas area; spurred states to begin enacting laws to protect infants from abandonment. Yet, even with these laws, babies continued to be found abandoned in unsafe places.

In Utah, the following horrific stories rocked that state in 2001. A days-old baby found dead in a dresser drawer. A child wrapped in a quilt and garbage sack and left in a park. Another drowned in a river and a fourth left in an irrigation pump house at a miniature golf course.

I stumbled on this story out of the Chicago area:

Mai Kwiatkowski had just returned to her Melrose Park home after a bad day at work when she heard a strange sound coming from behind her neighbor's home.

To the self-described animal lover, it sounded like an injured mourning dove, cooing. Kwiatkowski, 51, dropped her bags at her door Tuesday and went into the dark yard to have a look.

There Kwiatkowski found a newborn baby boy wrapped in a dirty purple woman's robe resting in a baby's carrier, crying and shuddering from the cold.

Kwiatkowski said she instinctively picked up the child and held him close. He was still warm. As she held him, he stopped crying. She called 911, all the while mumbling to herself in disbelief.

And this story out of Little Rock, Arkansas:

A Southwest Hospital nurse found an hours-old baby boy abandoned in a hospital restroom on a Sunday morning. The baby was the third abandoned infant found in the Little Rock area in as many months. Southwest Hospital nurse Connie Nichols found the child lying next to a trash bin in the women's third floor bathroom. The crying baby's umbilical cord was cut but not tied off, she said. Nichols found a note, written on a paper towel and lying on top of the infant, which said "This beautiful baby boy was born at six this morning. We are unable to care for it. Love, Mom and Dad." The child's parents have not been found.

Then I found this horrific story out of South Carolina:

New documents allege the baby was left in a toilet for seven hours before he was sealed in a black trash bag, placed in a trunk and later left in the church garbage can. The warrants suggest the baby boy was in the black bag for about an hour before he was rescued.

The mother told police she knew the baby was alive because he was crying, warrants say.

The mother, Maryuri Estefany Calix-Macedo, 21, remains in jail under an $800,000 bond.

A woman walking her dog heard the child's cries and found the baby in a sealed, black trash bag. The baby boy was bloody and had the umbilical cord still wrapped around his neck, but survived.

The warrants from police say the mother admitted she gave birth in the toilet at home in her bathroom. She told police she left the baby in the toilet for seven hours, until 4 p.m. on Thursday, July 16. After having the baby, she left the bathroom and went to feed her one-and-a-half year old daughter. Afterwards, she went back into the same bathroom, with her son still in the toilet, and took a shower.

Warrants say Macedo told officers she knew the baby was still alive at the time because she could hear him crying in the toilet.

The warrants say the baby was eventually placed in a black plastic trash bag that was tied shut and placed in the trunk of her car while she drove to Walmart to buy milk. Walmart video footage confirms Macedo and her daughter were inside the store for about 15 minutes. In her statement to police, Macedo says she knew the baby was still alive because she could hear him crying.

After she completed her shopping with the baby in the trunk, she drove to Christ Community Church, placed the sealed bag with the baby inside the blue trash bin and returned home.

Chicago news reports that the city keeps no statistics on the problem, but over the last two years children have been found abandoned in a shopping cart on the Near West Side, outside Sherman Hospital in South Elgin, in a bathroom at Westlake Community Hospital in Melrose Park and in the emergency room of Edward Hospital in Naperville. All were found alive.

And then I turned my focus to Indiana. The stories from my state alone left me devastated. The following three stories were out of Indianapolis. A male newborn was found deceased in Lick Creek. A man who was walking his dog, spotted something in the creek. Upon closer inspection, he realized it was a newborn. Another male infant was found in a dumpster located in the parking lot of an empty warehouse. The baby was wearing a diaper only. The mother has never been identified. And the third story was a male newborn found by a hospital employee near the entrance to the emergency room laying in a snowbank. The newborn was wrapped in a blanket decorated with baseballs and bats. Indianapolis police stated that the infant had a necklace around his neck and was wearing a homemade diaper. The hospital physician stated that it was impossible to revive the infant because his body was completely frozen.

In Lawrence, Indiana, a seventeen year old gave birth to a baby girl in her home; she wrapped the baby in a towel and placed her inside a shoe box. On her way to school, she placed the shoe box with the baby inside on an elderly lady's front porch. Inside the box with the baby was a note that said; "I can't take care of my baby, PLEASE HELP!" The newborn was found on the porch a couple hours later in 14 degree weather. She was taken to the hospital.

In Merrillville, Indiana, a newborn baby girl wrapped in a sweatshirt and placed in a box and was left on the porch of a Merrillville police officer. The officer's wife found the newborn on her porch. The baby still had its umbilical cord attached. They estimated the infant had been abandoned there a few hours prior to her discovery.

In North Vernon, Indiana, a newborn baby boy with his placenta still attached, was found wrapped in a blanket outside of a local church. The baby was suffering from dehydration and an infection. Authorities estimated the baby had been abandoned six hours earlier. What was especially mind-boggling, this church was right across the parking lot from a fire station.

And finally, in Lowell, Indiana, a newborn baby girl also with placenta still attached, was found in the backyard of a rural home by a 9-year-old girl. The infant was sunburned and had ants covering her face and body. Authorities estimated the baby was abandoned the night before she was discovered.

I could continue to fill these pages with stories of infants being drowned in a bathtub in a dorm room, or being thrown from the 5th story of an apartment building, as well as being left in a toilet in the restroom at prom. Devastating stories of desperate women who in a panic, made terrible choices for their babies and themselves. When you take a closer look at these stories, many infants were left near or on the property of legal safe haven locations. What were these mothers trying to tell us? They were petrified of face to face interaction. While the current Safe Haven Laws in all 50 states provided for "confidential" surrender, they were not anonymous surrenders. And in small towns when surrendering a newborn to a firefighter, paramedic, law enforcement personnel or hospital worker; the chances are extremely high that someone receiving custody of the surrendered infant would certainly KNOW this mother..

In the middle of all this research, as well as in the midst of my effort to create a non-profit, and research the creation of the baby box and legislation needed; I had a "God encounter". I met a woman by the name of Linda Znachko. Linda was passionate about the ministry that God had placed on her heart, and I was so impressed by her tenacity to honor and respect infants who had died without a name or proper burial.

The first dead baby Linda Znachko became involved with was found in a dumpster, wearing only a diaper.

She saw the news story about "Baby Doe," and what she particularly noted was that the public outrage was clearly leading people to ask what kind of mother would do such a thing and in what kind of society do such things occur. Linda wasn't caught up in that. As a mother of four, she just wanted to know what would happen next to the baby.

So Linda called the coroner's office. What she heard, she couldn't believe: Unclaimed babies were buried without ceremony, without names, in unmarked graves.

"I was appalled, that in the 21st century, in our country and in this city, that still happens," Linda told a reporter with The Indianapolis Star. One thought overpowered her: A dumpster is not a grave. A diaper is not burial clothing. Doe is not a name.

In October of 2009, Linda founded a ministry called "He Knows Your Name". She explained to me the day we met that sadly, even with the Safe Haven Law in Indiana, babies are still abandoned, buried in nameless graves, with no headstones to either mark their deaths, or more importantly, their LIVES. Linda was determined to ensure that every child received a name in life and dignity and honor in death. Our hearts were united in purpose in that very first meeting.

On December 29th, 2014, the following story appeared in the *Indianapolis Star:*

"Police are investigating the death of what appeared to be a newborn girl whose body was found Sunday afternoon at Eagle Creek Park on the northwest side.

The baby was found near the 8200 block of Wilson Road, about 30 yards from the parking lot. She was wrapped in a blue sweatshirt with a logo that says, "Aviation Maintenance Vincennes University-Indianapolis," according to the Indianapolis Metropolitan Police Department."

Linda jumped into action, she said she knew immediately that she had to help. She contacted the coroner's office, as she had done many times before, and made preparations to receive the infant girl as well as for a funeral and headstone as soon as they would release the baby to her. I asked Linda about the name she chose for this infant girl. Linda said she named her Amelia, because of the Aviation school logo on the sweatshirt she had been wrapped in. She further told me, "I knew this was the perfect name. Amelia means 'Defender', and when it is capitalized in scripture, that indicates it is an attribute of God. He is THE 'Defender', and I know that Amelia will be a defender of abandoned infants even in her death."

Amelia's middle name was given to her by Jessica, the tech who cared for her at the coroner's office. This poor girl was so traumatized by what she saw, what was left of this precious baby who had been ravaged by wild animals. Linda invited Jessica to give her a middle name and it rocked her world to have the privilege of joining us in naming her. Jessica chose the name Grace. When Linda asked her why Grace, Jessica said, she knew God showed it when Linda claimed her and honored her. Linda then asked her if she believed in God and she said, "not really...I now need to think about that!" Amelia's life touched so many right from the beginning!

Because Linda was aware of my crusade to bring baby boxes to Indiana and beyond and to ensure no baby dies from abandonment ever again, she allowed me to also help name this abandoned baby. I decided on the name Hope. I wanted people to understand that even in the midst of this tragedy, we can still find Hope from this precious baby. So today her headstone reads: Amelia Grace Hope.

A month later, I invited Linda to testify in front of the Senate Committee in Indiana and as she gave her powerful testimony she distributed to everyone a copy of baby Amelia's footprint that the funeral director had given her earlier. I sat in that committee room amazed at this piece of paper I was holding. I kept staring at it, almost like I did with the Delta napkin on that Delta flight returning from South Africa. I knew this footprint was going to be extremely significant for us and I told myself that day, I had to honor this baby in some way.

God's timing is always on point. The next day I was meeting with our graphic designer, Wally, who was finalizing our logo for my new non-profit. I arrived at his office with this "footprint" paper in my hand and I said "Let's scratch the logo that we've been working on for the last two months, I want to make this footprint the focal point of the logo." Understand, he has no idea about the origin of this tiny footprint, but he scanned it in and started configuring concepts of the footprint around the words "Safe Haven Baby Boxes". At one point, he began to start coloring the footprint in and I immediately went off. "What are you doing? You can't fill this footprint in. Rescan it and start over!" Wally was completely confused so I proceeded to tell him the story of the footprint. The logo you see for Safe Haven Baby Boxes today, is the footprint of baby Amelia, unedited!

Amelia's footprint, emblazoned in our logo, stands in defense of the hundreds of infants abandoned in Indiana and across our country. It also brings Hope that many more infants will be safely surrendered, adopted and loved in the years ahead.

If you are still with me and haven't put the book down, thank you. This is hard. It was hard for me to research, it was painful to read and it was even more painful to revisit and write this chapter. But this is so important! We cannot choose to live in ignorance, we cannot afford to turn away. These were precious children, created in the image of God. They were, each and everyone of them, loved by Jesus. Their lives mattered! They deserve to be given dignity, they deserve honor. And they desperately deserve to have their voices heard.

I was determined to give honor and a voice to these precious infants. Amelia's voice would not be silenced, and her death would not be in vain. Everytime I look at her little footprint on the logo of every business card I hand out, every letter or email I send, I am reminded of why I fight so hard. I will speak for them, until I am no longer able to speak and there is no breath left in me.

If you are ready to join me, and DO something, not just sit in your sorrow for these babies, then buckle up my friend! We're about to take a ride!!!

Chapter 6

MAKING THE VISION REALITY

"Imagine all the host of Heaven watching with bated breath wondering what you will do next. Your life matters, and the choices you make matter. Nothing about you is inconsequential. Live with purpose." -Billy Graham

It is one thing to have a vision, another to have passion for your purpose, and yet a whole new challenge to get that vision and dream out of your head, onto paper and birthed into reality. This was the task ahead of me. Once again, on a bigger piece of paper than that Delta napkin, I had to make a checklist, my very long "to-do" list, that threatened to overwhelm.

1. Set up a Non-profit: create a name, file paperwork with IRS and build a Board of Directors.

2. Build the BOX: Complete Design from Fabrication to Electronics to Manufacturing and everything in between.

3. Find a lawyer and experts in legislation to make the use of the box a legal surrender in the state of Indiana.

4. Build an Education and Awareness campaign

5. Develop a 24 hour National Safe Haven Crisis Hotline

6. Build a Donor Base, research grants and foundations and develop strong partnerships

My head was exploding. I believe that in that moment, I fully understood how Peter felt in the Gospels. You remember that story, Peter and the other disciples were on the stormy waters of the Sea of Galilee, afraid for their lives, and through the storm they saw a man walking toward them on the water. Peter called out and said, "If it is you Jesus, tell me to walk out to you on the water" and Jesus replied "Come". Of course, Peter just got right out of that boat and began walking. Most of us only remember that this is the part of the story where Peter sunk into the waves. He took his eyes off of Jesus, and put his eyes on the danger and the storm, and immediately began sinking. Jesus reached his hands out to Peter, and said "Why did you doubt?"

Two important lessons here, the first is be brave enough to get out of the boat! There were 12 disciples, eleven of them "boat huggers" and only ONE "water walker"! I answered the call to get out of that boat, as scary as it was and alone as I felt! The second lesson is "Keep your eyes on Jesus, not the waves!" This is where I found myself on this particular part of the journey. Was I going to be overwhelmed by the task at hand, would I give up when the storm became too much, or would I keep my eyes on Jesus and walk on water?

I have learned that the key to tackling a task this big, or running a race this strenuous, is to put one foot in front of the other and take that first step. And after that first step, continue to take the next, and the next and the next. I dove in.

I filed all of the paperwork for our 501(c)3 and named the organization "Safe Haven Baby Boxes". I had a huge board of directors; My husband, Pam Stenzel and Me! You have to start somewhere!

When I began to tackle the task of design, I reached out to a fellow firefighter, Jason Mueller, who owned a company in Fort Wayne called Fabcore Industries. I will never forget his face when I showed up to sell my project and concept to him. I wish I had a picture of his expression, the shock and confusion clearly visible on his face as I told him I needed a box built to install in the wall of a fire station in which to place a newborn. We just stood there, staring at each other, when he finally said, "You want to do what? And put it where?" "I'll build you anything you want for $700 dollars" he stated, and I handed him a check from my husband's bank account and walked out the door like a boss!!.

While he still believed I was completely out of my mind, he accepted the challenge and he and his team at Fabcore began working on the design and creating a prototype based on the drawing on that delta napkin. I still have the very first prototype he created, the box that I carted all over the state of Indiana, including right up to the State House. It will forever hold a special place in my heart. Jason and Fabcore Industries still build our baby boxes today.

I also enlisted the help of a wonderful electrical engineer, Rick. He agreed to design all of the electronics that would lock the outside door after it closed and set off all three alarms to let 911 know that a baby was placed in the box. We designed 3 separate alarms, one when the door to the box was opened, another when there was movement inside the box, and the third was a button inside the door that a mother could push setting off the final silent alarm. Even though that third alarm was probably unnecessary for emergency services, I felt it was an important step for the person surrendering. It was an opportunity to say "I am making this decision", intentionally choosing, to keep that baby safe. When she shuts that door, it locks. This is an important safety feature. We also have an alarm that notifies personnel if the baby box ever loses power. This was also a very important safety feature as the baby box has to have power to run properly. The infant can only be retrieved by a firefighter or hospital staff from the inside of the building. Our initial protocol was that the infant should be retrieved within 5 minutes of the first alarm. We have never gone over that time limit, and in most instances we are well under the 3 minute mark.

Finally, I contacted Smithworks Medical in Texas. Smithworks is another company founded by a firefighter, Douglas M. Smith. He was working as an EMT in Northwest Oregon, and because of the climate in that region, they were placing IV fluids on the defroster vents in the ambulance to warm them up on the way to a call. Realizing that nothing was being done to effectively warm IV fluids in the prehospital arena, he set out to change that. He developed and built iv fluid warmers for fire and ambulance services. When I contacted Mr. Smith and shared our "baby box" project with him and the need to control the temperature inside the box, he immediately jumped on board and built the device used in our initial boxes to keep them cool in the heat and warm in the cold of winter.

Some of you may be interested in more detail on the design and operation of the box itself, and for the sake of space and time, we have placed detailed information and even video illustration of the box and it's operation on the website that accompanies this book. Please take the time to check it out and learn more about this amazing device that is saving the lives of infants at risk for abandonment.

Simultaneously, I needed expert legal advice and needed a legislator who would be willing to help lead the process of getting the state statute to reflect the use of the baby box. Fortunately I had a great friend, Cathie Humbarger, who is a giant in the prolife movement and Executive Director of Allen County Right to Life. In May of 2014, she introduced me to Casey Cox, a local attorney and state legislator who was very interested in the state's current Safe Haven Law and understanding why it appeared that it was under utilized. Casey was planning to research the issue over the summer and then get together and brainstorm more effective ways to see infant abandonment end in Indiana. Casey was instrumental in drafting the legislation and navigating HB1016 through the state house. The Bill reads as follows:

> Newborn safety incubators. Requires the commission on improving the status of children in Indiana to submit, before January 1, 2016, to the general assembly and the governor's office recommendations concerning: (1) new methods or mechanisms for carrying out policies relating to abandoned children; and (2) the production and distribution of information and posting of uniform signs regarding certain laws regarding emergency custody of abandoned children. Requires the state department of health to prepare and submit, before January 1, 2016, to the general assembly and the governor's office recommendations concerning standards and protocols for the installation and operation of newborn safety.
>
> https://legiscan.com/IN/bill/HB1016/2015

This bill, authored by Representative Cox, had its first reading on January 6, 2015. You can view the entire journey this legislation took on the Indiana State legislative website. The bill made its way through the House and Senate and back to the House. It was eventually signed by the Speaker, then the President of the Senate, culminating with the signature of then Governor Mike Pence on April 27th, 2015. (For the sake of space in this book and in an attempt to not bore you with details, you can access the record by going to our companion web page.) I spent countless hours traveling between Woodburn, Indiana and Indianapolis. I carried our heavy prototype of the baby box, in and out of committee meetings, hearings and learned more about the legislative process than I ever thought I would know. It has left me with great respect for those who patiently fight for the lives of children every session, year in and year out. It was truly an honor to partner with Representative Casey Cox and the many other representatives and senators who would co sponsor our legislation.

The day we went down to Indianapolis and had the privilege of being present when Governor Mike Pence signed the legislation into law, is a day I will never forget. So many of our supporters and those who had made this day possible were able to join us. That day felt like a huge victory, even though it would soon be clear that the battle to provide a safe and truly anonymous option for surrendering a newborn had only just begun!

Pam Stenzel and I had many conversations both in South Africa, and in the days and weeks following, about the need for education, awareness and the importance of operating a National Hotline. Pam has extensive experience working in the crisis pregnancy care arena, including having been the executive director of Alpha Women's Center in the suburbs of Minneapolis, Minnesota; and currently working for the Community Pregnancy Clinics of Florida. Pam had trained hotline workers in the area of crisis pregnancy help, and knew that it would be important that mothers in crisis had the ability to reach out by calling or text, to get information in a crisis. It's not enough to just install boxes in buildings, if no one knows that they exist. We had already experienced the reality that even though the state of Indiana had a law that made surrendering a newborn at a hospital or fire station was legal, the Department of Children Services had spent absolutely no money….zero….nada on education and awareness. How do you expect young mothers to utilize this option as a last resort if they don't know the option is available to them! And so, with Pam's help and guidance we launched our 24 Hotline: 1-866-99BABY1.

I began speaking in schools and in churches and in any setting I was invited, to bring awareness to the Safe Haven Law. We launched an extensive social media campaign, which has grown tremendously. I learned how to blog and tweet and even operate "Facebook Live" as well as a variety of other vehicles to get the word out and reach that critical age group most at risk for infant abandonment. We printed brochures, bookmarks, magnets, T-shirts, bumper stickers and anything we thought might help us get the word out about the hotline while we worked to finish the process of getting the boxes installed in fire stations. At this point, I was wearing so many hats, my neck was breaking! Marketer, Speaker, Lobbyist, Grant writer, CEO, engineer, firefighter/medic and Mom! All the while, with the exception of the paycheck from being a medic/firefighter, my paycheck was a smile, and those didn't come all that often, but I smile alot more knowing that!

With all of these plates spinning in the air, I now needed to figure out how we were going to fund this massive project. I knew my husband wasn't going to keep letting me dip into his checking account. We desperately needed funding if we were going to see these boxes become a reality. I was able to secure a few small grants from foundations in Indiana, but we were going to need stronger partnerships.

I was asked to speak at an event for The Gabriel Project in Indianapolis. I was seated at a table with a few members of the Knights of Columbus in Indiana, Mike and Scott. I had met Mike earlier in the evening, but this was the first time I had the opportunity to meet Scott, who was the Grand Knight for the State of Indiana. Scott was clearly moved by my testimony and my passion for the Safe Haven Baby Box program, which was just in the legislative pipeline at the time. When I was done speaking, he asked a multitude of questions. Scott revealed to me that he was an adopted child himself, and had a special place in his heart for adoption and adoptive families.

At the end of his list of questions, he asked me "What do you need?"

I started to reply with the little things, help with education, awareness, materials, billboards, etc. and he stopped me. "No, what do you NEED?" Mike tried to provide insight, "He's talking about money." Let me insert here, I am not familiar AT ALL with the Knights of Columbus at this point, I had absolutely no idea who they were, and certainly had no clue about the important position Scott held within the organization. Because it was fresh on my mind, I blurted out "Well, I did pay $700 for this prototype and it would be nice to have that reimbursed." Scott replied, "That's a good start, we will certainly talk more". I went home that night and proudly informed my husband that I had met a very nice gentleman by the name of Scott Knight who lived in Columbus Indiana and he was going to donate $700. We have had a great laugh over that announcement since! By the way, his name is Scott and he doesn't live in Columbus, Indiana.

The relationship with the Indiana Knights of Columbus became absolutely critical in the beginning months and years of Safe Haven Baby Boxes. It was a privilege to have Scott and his wife Chanel present with Governor Mike Pence when HB1016 was signed into law. Scott invited me to speak at the state Convention that spring and the response of the Knights who attended was so encouraging. Many of them were so moved by my story and my mission that they committed to do everything they could to bring a Baby Box to their respective communities. Every Baby Box installed to this date has the handprint of the Knights of Columbus all over it. Not simply monetary help in funding the box itself, but help with installation, alarm company costs, awnings, billboards and even building sidewalks leading up to the box itself. And the wives of the Knights have been instrumental in sewing mattress covers and even the curtains that hang on the inside of the Fire Station on the baby box giving privacy to the bassinet. My mom designed and created the first mattress covers, then shared the dimensions with the Knights and these lovely women have made every mattress cover since that time. Every box gets a minimum of two mattress covers.

I will forever cherish the relationship I have with the Knights of Columbus and the support that they have given me and the Safe Haven Baby Box organization from the very beginning. I have spoken at many state conventions as well as travelled all over the state of Indiana and beyond, to speak with individual councils. One of the most memorable, if you can call it that, experiences I have had with the Knights was following one of the banquets at the state convention. I was standing in the back of the ballroom, just talking with members when a woman came running in yelling for my help! She said someone had collapsed and they needed immediate medical attention. I ran out to the hallway and there was a woman laying on the floor, gasping for air. I immediately fell into "medic mode" and asked for scissors and any emergency equipment available from the hotel. I knew the EMT's were on their way and that I had to prep her for them to arrive, all the while praying she didn't completely stop breathing and go into cardiac arrest. I began cutting off her clothes and fortunately the hotel had an AED (automated external defibrillator) and immediately began to slap the pads onto her chest in case her heart stopped beating. I continued to monitor her pulse praying for EMS to arrive quickly as things were starting to turn south. In the middle of the panic, Scott had gotten a hold of blankets somehow and was valiantly attempting to shield her for privacy. The EMT's arrived and I gave them some history of what happened and what I knew and they transported her to the hospital with lights and sirens. We later learned that she had experienced a brain aneurysm and are so grateful that with immediate care, she has made almost a full recovery. We are all called to protect life, at every stage and at every moment!

Later in this book I will fill in details about the installation of the various boxes as well as the amazing stories of babies who have been protected, adopted and loved as a result of our efforts. But I wanted to end this chapter by acknowledging others who have come alongside my efforts over the past few years. Our Board of Directors has grown to 9, and each member has a special heart and task that make these efforts possible.

My dear friend, Kristi Hofferber, was the first to join the small board of three and make it four. Kristi has an amazing testimony, as she was conceived in incest. Her grandfather is her "father", and her biological mother endured years of abuse and multiple abortions before she escaped her abuser, who was her own father. Kristi tells of the heroic way her mother hid her pregnancy in order to escape the abuse and eventually delivered Kristi and placed her with an adoptive family. Kristi is now a pastor's wife in Southwestern Illinois, and the mother of two adopted children. She was such a gift to us in the beginning stages of developing Safe Haven Baby Boxes and has become a close friend.

We added my birth cousin, Teresa Bertke and her husband Don. Teresa and Don are both firefighters and their input and support have been invaluable. And what an extra plus to have a member of my birth family actively involved in making this vision a reality. It always reminds me of the goodness of God and His plan.

I received a call one day from a woman who told me she had read about our efforts in a news story and wanted to know more and really wanted to join our efforts. She informed me that she was the current "Mrs. Wyoming" and would be competing in the International pageant soon and wanted to make Safe Haven Baby Boxes part of her platform. Priscilla Pruitt joined our board and has helped immensely in bringing national and international awareness to our efforts. Priscilla has been a fantastic spokesperson for the safe haven law as well as the baby box program. Priscilla is bi-lingual and has helped us translate much of our material and signage into spanish. Priscilla and her husband Sean have been invaluable members of our team. It was awesome to watch Priscilla win the Mrs. International title in 2016.

Kevin Albin was added to our team, first as a volunteer and finally as a board member. Kevin's tireless help with our social media outreach and even being the "last resort" hotline help if the other counselors are on other calls, has been invaluable. He has handled the onslaught of Facebook and Instagram messages and inquiries. He has spent countless hours keeping communication lines open for both supporters and those who might need help.

Finally, we have rounded out our board of directors with an amazing Fire Chief, Pascal Arnes. Chief Arnes has been an invaluable link between Safe Haven Baby Boxes and the community of Fire Fighters.

This has been a monumental journey, but it has boosted my faith as I have witnessed God's provision at every step. Just the breadth of the task, looking back, is enough to shock me. No journey is without it's conflict. No one has ever attempted to follow the path on which God places you, without meeting resistance. The enemy doesn't need to bother with soldiers who are not on the battlefield. I have determined to be the kind of woman that when my feet hit the floor in the morning, the devil says "Oh crap, she's up."

I know that I have not been alone on this path and that God's provision for every need, even in miraculous ways, will give me strength to journey on. I pray that you, too, know that He will never abandon you! Hang on to that promise!

Chapter 7

HERE COMES THE STORM

"Adversity, which looks and feels like such a determined enemy, can become a valuable ally. Only you can decide which it will be." – Joni Eareckson Tada

If you thought the only obstacle to seeing my vision become reality was the enormity of the task in front of me, you would be sadly mistaken. As big as that mountain I had to climb was, I had to climb it with the violent storm of attacks from bureaucracy, supposed allies and one mentally unstable but persistent detractor. Nothing worth fighting for comes without the fight, and though I knew there would be opposition, I totally underestimated its brute force. They say "what doesn't kill you makes you stronger", believe me when I say that I now have the strength of the incredible hulk!

The battles started immediately, and I had to take all of them on simultaneously. After the safe haven legislation was signed into law and the baby box became a legal form of surrender in the state of Indiana, we began to get push back from the Department of Children Services and other state government agencies. The legislation that we passed specifically tasked the Indiana Department of Health with creating protocols, policies and procedures for the baby box. With little opposition from DHS or DCS during the legislative session of 2015, suddenly the Department of Health just refused to do their job. They were not tasked with researching the validity or necessity of the device, they were simply tasked with coming up with Policies and Procedures for the installation, and use of the baby box. Because they refused to do their job, Safe Haven Baby Boxes did it for them. With the help of our attorneys, we came up with our own extensive Protocols,

Policies and Procedures. Also, with the help of three different law firms across the state of Indiana, whose opinion clearly stated that installing boxes in hospitals and fire stations was perfectly legal without the Department of Health protocols, we proceeded to install two boxes. The first box was installed in my home Fire Station in Woodburn, Indiana on April 26, 2016. Now just to give you a little back story, my husband was the Mayor at the time so it was rather easy to talk him into allowing me to do this if he ever wanted to sleep in a warm bed with his wife again. The second box was installed two days later in the Coolspring Volunteer Fire Department in the northwest corner of Indiana. We chose that location because there had been several illegal abandonments of infants very near that particular location. We knew that the entire corridor between Chicago and Michigan needed the baby boxes.

Suddenly, Indiana's bureaucrats "care" about abandoned infants? After doing absolutely nothing to promote or market the existing safe haven law for over 15 years, the Deputy Director of Communication for DCS, James Wide, decides to make public their opposition to Safe Haven Baby Boxes. Let's put this in context, Indiana's Commission on Improving the Status of Children and the Indiana Task Force on Infant Mortality and Child Health don't condone the use of the Safe Haven Baby Box because, quite frankly, they don't care. We should ALL agree resources should be spent in promoting the Safe Haven laws in Indiana. More importantly, it **SHOULD** come from the Indiana Health Department and Department of Child Services. Unfortunately, in the two years that Safe Haven Baby Boxes had been in operation, Safe Haven Baby Boxes had spent in excess of $25,000 on advertising and marketing the Safe Haven Baby Box and Crisis Hotline. In 2016 alone, there had been 942 calls to the hotline with 132 crisis pregnancy referrals, 4 adoption referrals and 6 face to face facilitated surrenders by Safe Haven Baby Boxes. The State of Indiana up to this point has spent $0 (zero) dollars promoting Indiana Safe Haven laws, but now decides to spend countless hours and tens of thousands of dollars fighting Safe Haven Baby Boxes? As I wrote to the Journal Gazette in 2016, "As Hoosiers, we should be appalled at the misappropriation of funds and resources coming from a department that has an $800,000,000 (That's 800 million, just shy of a billion) budget, with Indiana languishing in the bottom 20% of states for infant mortality. We call on the Indiana Health Department and Department of Child Services to join us in focusing on our most vulnerable Hoosiers, mothers-in-crisis and their infants." But not only did they refuse to focus on our most vulnerable citizens, they continued to fight my little non-profit that was trying to save lives!

Shortly after we installed Baby Box #1 in Woodburn, and Baby Box #2 in Coolspring township, Mary Beth Bonaventura, at the time serving as head of the Department of Children Services publicly threatened to take legal action against us and tried to force us to shut down the box program. In a statement to WANE news she said the following:

"We would have to file legal action to bring a temporary restraining order or something like that and the court would hear both sides and determine whether or not it should operate in the manner they're operating in," Bonaventura said. "I don't think we should put babies in a box and Indiana law does not allow us to do that and not be prosecuted civilly and criminally."

She further stated in that same interview that she hoped there was no future in the state of Indiana for the boxes and that there was no proof that abandonments would go down. Interesting, because at the time of the writing of this book, some 4 years later, there has not been one deadly abandonment of a newborn in the state of Indiana, while across the country there have been hundreds of illegal and deadly abandonments in the same time frame. I guess Ms. Bonaventura is more interested in her opinion than she is in empirical data.

And to make matters worse, these bureaucrats continued their crusade against our boxes at the state house. Indiana Department of Children's Services, represented by Ms. Parvonay, made multiple false statements at a legislative hearing in 2016. Ms. Parvonay first tried to claim that our boxes were untested. This was completely false, as our boxes had undergone rigorous testing for 15 months prior to that hearing and at the time were being independently tested by a company out of Ohio. She then tried to claim that the Safe Haven Law was working because there had been 33 safe surrenders since the law had been enacted. What she failed to mention, clearly not an oversite, was that in that same time frame 38 infants had been illegally dumped in trash cans in our state. Did she attempt to mislead the legislators by not mentioning the fact that more infants had been dumped than had been safely surrendered? Did she know how many of those 38 precious babies died? Did DCS even bother to track the number of illegal abandonments? On what basis did she feel she could emphatically state that the law was working? And by the way, how many of those 33 safe surrenders were a direct result of calls to our hotline, paid for by my non profit, and staffed by my volunteers? How in the world can we as citizens and those who care for the most vulnerable among us, purport that we care when we don't even bother to look honestly at what is broken in our system and make every attempt to fix it? We certainly celebrate the 33 mothers who did the right thing and safely surrendered their newborns, but we must not forget the 38 mothers who did not!

During the Fall of 2016, while Mary Beth Bonaventura and the other bureaucrats at the Department of Children Services were fighting us every step of the way, we were happy to announce to the legislature that since we had installed our baby boxes (at that time there were only two) and still to this very day, there have been ZERO deadly abandonments in our state. That my friends, is the statistic that should matter!

It should also be noted that since installation of the first boxes in April of 2016, they have been tested weekly and have never failed, not even once. I have personally trained hundreds of firefighters and first responders across Indiana and in the fire stations that have installed a baby box there has never been a response time greater than 5 minutes. Compare that to the number of babies who were found hours or sadly even days after being left outside hospitals, fire stations or even worse being left in dumpsters or trash bins. Which outcome is preferable? A mother leaving her newborn in the bed of a parked pickup truck outside of a fire station, hoping that someone will find that baby before he freezes to death or a mother who is desperate for anonymity to open one of our temperature controlled, safe baby boxes that will send out an alarm and have first responders retrieve that infant in under 5 minutes? I am still completely flabbergasted that those who claim to care about the lives and safety of children have a hard time answering that question!

While going to battle with Indiana State bureaucrats, I suddenly had to deal with the national safe haven leadership. Up until April of 2016, I had enjoyed a fairly good relationship with the National Safe Haven Alliance and its volunteers. This loosely formed organization was made up of people, who for the most part, cared about the Safe Haven Laws in their respective states and wanted to see infant abandonment come to an end. I spoke frequently with Heather, who worked with the Arizona Safe Baby Haven Foundation, and we discussed the "baby drawers" being utilized in hospitals in Arizona. The only other state in the United States that was utilizing a "device" as part of a legal Safe Haven Surrender that offered 100% anonimity. I even flew to Arizona, where Heather welcomed me, took me to breakfast and then showed me the "baby drawers" and explained how they operated in the hospitals in Phoenix. She even worked hard to make their protocols, policies and procedures for the baby drawers when they were first installed since she worked for the hospital chain that was installing them.

We spoke often after that meeting and were in agreement that education was paramount, and that if women were going to surrender legally, face to face, or with a baby drawer or baby box, they needed to be aware of all of their options. We discussed different strategies for getting that education out there to a broader audience and the operation of the Safe Haven Baby Box 24 hour hotline. Our organization's hotline is managed by a professional counselor, who had over 25 years of experience in the crisis pregnancy field and had operated multiple hotlines for women experiencing a crisis pregnancy. Heather was interested initially, in training those who answered their hotline as most were good hearted volunteers, but with no formal training.

I also had maintained a good relationship with Tim, a retired Ambulance Medical Technician from Nassau County, NY. Tim was one of the founding members of the National Safe Haven Alliance and was very encouraging and helpful in the initial stages of founding Safe Haven Baby Boxes and our efforts in the state of Indiana. I even sent Tim a copy of the original legislation to review. He told me he would share the legislation with his board of directors and get back to me. I received an email back a few weeks later, it was short and sweet and simply said:" Hi Monica, we looked at it and it is good. Tim".

And then the wrecking ball came crashing into our positive momentum. A man by the name of Michael Morrisey decided to become my worst nightmare. He single handedly wreaked havoc on absolutely every facet of Safe Haven Baby Boxes, including attacks on every person associated with us both personally and professionally. It was mind blowing. How in the world did this one person have the time and energy to stalk all of us incessantly? He clearly spends every waking moment of his life obsessed with me, stalking me, and Safe Haven Baby Boxes!

For some background, Mike Morrisey was a founding member of the National Safe Haven Alliance and the self proclaimed head of a "not for profit" organization in Massachusetts called "Baby Safe Haven of New England". This organization is not a legal entity and per Jeff Williams, with the Corporations Division of Massachusetts, "Baby Safe Haven of New England" had its non-profit status "involuntary revoked" on June 8, 2012. Morrisey has absolutely no qualifications, education or experience that would make him an "expert" on infant abandonment or the safe haven law. Unlike others in the movement who are first responders, medical and mental health professionals, Mr. Morrisey is a "self proclaimed" talent agent and photographer who solicits teen girls. In order to further his "talent agency" and his access to underage children, Mr. Morrisey decided to pose as an interested party in the Safe Haven movement. Shortly after beginning his relentless and personal attack on me, my family and my organization, he was removed from the National Safe Haven board of directors. This did not stop his attacks, and incrediously, many of the board members who had previously been supportive or at a minimum neutral when it came to baby boxes, decided to fight us and our efforts alongside Mr. Morrisey. How anyone could take his accusations and relentless personal attacks seriously is beyond me.

Initially we thought we could just politely answer his ridiculous accusations and ignore him altogether, but we were sadly mistaken. He was determined to ruin Safe Haven Baby Boxes, me personally and anyone associated with the organization. He went after board members, including Priscilla Pruitt, who was at the time competing for the Mrs. International title. Just prior to her competition in the pageant, he wrote scathing letters to pageant officials and accused Priscilla of lying and promoting an illegitimate nonprofit "scam". He wrote relentlessly to the International headquarters of the Knights of Columbus, again threatening to expose their support of the "scam" of baby boxes if they did not cease their financial support of the baby box program. He went after Fabcore Industries by communicating with it's insurer, trying to get their insurance cancelled. He sent letters accusing us of being "charlatans", "scammers", operating unsafe and untested medical devices". In one of his nefarius emails to the Knights of Columbus he stated the following:

> "the Indiana Knights of Columbus are going to spend a quarter million dollars on a program that leads women to secret back alley deliveries, then to place their newborn babies that may be in great distress into a converted pig feeding trough in an unmanned fire station. These so called "baby boxes" are made as pig feeding bins, with a few electronics attached."

He harassed us on social media constantly posting lies and misinformation. He would friend request anyone on Facebook who posted anything about Safe Haven Baby Boxes and proceed to barrage them with hateful accusations. We had to encourage all of our supporters and anyone associated with us in any way, to block him immediately. This didn't stop him from creating fake accounts and attempting to continue to stalk us.

He stalked every organization that invited me to speak at their events. He sent the following to Rose Mimms, the executive director of Arkansas Right to Life:

> "Are you still going to have the so-called "baby boxes" "advocate" as a speaker for your event? […] If this scam speaks in front of your group you will become part of the scam, and you will never be trusted with a single safe haven law awareness action. We will alert the proper Arkansas agencies with all the evidence of your scam, along with the "baby boxes" scam artist who works with you. […] Please

dump this speaker from your event, or be ready for her continuous lies. Proper Baby Safe Haven groups will do work for Arkansas, and AK Right to Life will have NOTHING to do with it if you attempt to follow this scam artist."

Yes I know, Arkansas is AR but this is an exact excerpt from his letter, which goes to show the astounding IQ of Mr. Morrisey who clearly doesn't realize that AK stands for Alaska.

Throughout this entire time, Morrisey not only harassed anyone and any organization associated with Safe Haven Baby Boxes, he began personally threatening me and my family. When you start messing with this momma's kids, you can bet the claws came out! I had to contact the Woodburn Police Department because of his threats to me and my family. He then proceeded to call the police department constantly (18 times to be exact in one night) demanding that I be arrested and then threatening the police officer! Clearly, he had completely lost his mind!

When it seemed his antics were getting him nowhere, he issued a "press release" from his illegal non profit that read as follows:

"Indiana has been taken over by an overbearing 50 year old "advocate" who hogs every single media spotlight to the insistence that there never be a teen/20s advocate to replace her, and her ill-fated "baby boxes" concept. The losses of life, the ruining of lives, it's all about marketing, and Indiana is doing it in the worst possible way with the "baby boxes" advocate hoarding the spotlights every single time."

I could fill this entire chapter with his incoherent ramblings, I won't bore you. We filed a lawsuit against him in Indiana. It was a complaint for 'Defamation'; 'Tortious Interference with business Relationships'; 'Intentional Interference with Contractual Relations; "Negligent Infliction of Emotional Distress; and Intentional Infliction of Emotional Distress." After a long and drawn out fight in court, we won our case against Morrisey, his wife Jean and "Baby Safe Haven of New England". The judge ordered the Morriseys to pay $25,000 to Safe Haven Baby Boxes and he also issued a lifetime injunction against them to ensure our safety. A year after this verdict we filed contempt charges against him for violating the injunction 108 times and the judge held him in contempt and slapped another fine on him of $15,000. You would think this would be the end of his harassment, but you would be wrong. It seemed to only embolden him and even cause him to step up the insanity of his accusations and insults. The harassment, stalking and intimidation continue to this day.

Establishing Mike Morrisey as a deranged lunatic with nothing better to do with his life than harass, threaten and obsess over me and my organization is easy, but understanding how this psychopath could influence seemingly sane individuals who claim to care about infant abandonment and saving lives, to join in his delusion is puzzling. Why would personnel with the National Safe Haven Alliance and others choose to distance themself from Morrisey, and then turn around and join in the harassment and negative threats? Tim went as far as to produce a hilarious Youtube video (it truly looks like a bad SNL skit) where he tried to insinuate that the boxes weren't "safe" being installed in a Fire Station because a terrorist might use them to plant a bomb. Really? If a terrorist was truly intent on harming first responders, all he would have to do is call 911 and we will roll right up to him and walk straight into their trap!

Despite these attacks and the harassment from Indiana bureaucrats, National Safe Haven advocates and one deranged lunatic, we pressed on! I was determined that I would not allow outside negative forces to deter me in my mission or to keep us from offering this last resort option to women in crisis. We were answering thousands of calls on our hotline, and assisting with more than 50 legal safe surrenders in Indiana and across the country. Babies' lives were being saved and women were being spared prosecution and jail time. As much as the enemy would have loved for me to give up and quit and turn my back on my calling, this warrior was never giving up! Never! The storm however, continued.

Chapter 8

THE STORM COMES HOME

"This storm will pass. Although, it has tested our strength, our foundations, our roots, we will arise stronger, wiser, and smarter. The best is yet to come."

—*Charles F Glassman*

Battling the "outside" world was a struggle, as well as tackling the continued inner struggle of finding purpose in pain. But nothing fully prepared me for the storm that was coming. Be assured of this, when you are fulfilling God's call on your life, and you are making a difference, the enemy will always come after you. If he can't get you to give up by using outside forces, he will most always change his tactics, and hit you the hardest where it matters most. The "storm" will hit your family!

It was 1:52 am on May 26, 2016 and my fire department pager was piercing the dark quiet of my bedroom, jolting me out of my sleep. There was a jeep rollover with a patient pinned under the vehicle. I jumped out of bed and grabbed my clothes from the floor. It was my habit every night that I was on duty, I would place my clothes by my bed so that if the pager goes off, which it usually does, I would be able to throw on my clothes and get out the door faster. I threw on my clothes, grabbed my cell phone and shoes and ran down the stairs and out to the truck.

Just as I was getting into my truck, I looked around and failed to see the black jeep that my son, JJ, was test driving the night before. I glanced over at the road, and observed the pick up truck that JJ's best friend Casey had driven over to our house earlier. JJ had explained to me that he was going to drive this jeep today so he could get it ready for the owner to sell. The owner was a friend of JJ's and had agreed to allow JJ to drive it around town and make sure that it was mechanically in good shape. I quickly shrug off the worries and head down to the station.

I pull up to my usual spot and put my truck in park. Jumping out, I grabbed my phone and my shoes. I quickly hop into the ambulance on the passenger side, while at the same time my partner, Zach, is climbing in on the driver's side. Zach asked, "is this accident on the old 24 or the new 24"? "Radio dispatch said the old 24," I told him. The overhead door is still going up, once it reaches the top, Zach turns on the lights and sirens, and we drive out of the station.

I needed to get my shoes on, I always leave that last for some reason. While bending over to put my shoes on, I began to get my head into the zone of what we could find when we arrived on scene and what equipment I would need when I jumped out of the ambulance. After accomplishing getting both shoes on and tied, I sat back up in the seat, and I happened to notice a significant amount of traffic heading from the direction of the accident. Let me explain, our little town of Woodburn, Indiana has a population of under 2000. This is a Wednesday night, actually early Thursday morning, and most people should be in bed. But for some unknown reason, the road is full of traffic, and I mentioned it to Zach. "Does this seem like a lot of cars for this early in the morning to you?" Zach replies, "yeah, a shit ton of cars."

My brain is still working over every possible scenario we could encounter once on scene. I want to be absolutely sure that we have everything we will need before I get out of this truck. As a medic, you start thinking of scenarios that could happen, and you go through the specific steps in your mind to help you determine what equipment you're going to need to grab when you get there. I knew this was a traumatic accident, so I was well aware that there would be some pretty significant life-threatening injuries.

"Emergency 165 this is Emergency 265 direct", the radio rang out. "Emergency 265 this is Emergency 165 go ahead," I stated. "Emergency 165, this is at my station "H" as my niece and nephew had some friends over tonight and had a bonfire. When you arrive on the scene, you need to stay in the right part of the driveway and follow it all the way back to the end of the fence and then turn left, and you should see the fire." "Emergency 165,

I'm clear on your traffic".

My cell phone is ringing, and I pick it up off the console, I see that it is JJ calling. I look at Zach, "It's just JJ being nosy." JJ often calls me when he sees fire trucks traveling down the road. "Hey JJ, what's up," as I answered the phone. "Mom, you have to hurry," JJ said. I replied, "JJ, are you involved in this accident?" "Mom hurry," JJ screamed into the phone. "JJ, are you ok," I asked? "Mom hurry," JJ yelled. I repeated, louder this time, "JJ, are you alright, JJ, are you ok, JJ answer me!" Zach, he isn't responding to me. "JJ answer me, are you ok"? The phone dropped the call, and I immediately dialed his number back, but there was no answer. I am in the middle of redialing his number, and our radio dispatch comes across the airways "Emergency 165, just for your information, CPR is now in progress". My heart just hit the floor, and I placed my forehead on the palm of my hand. "Zach, you need to hurry," I said. "This truck won't go any faster," he reminded me as I continued to panic.

My mind is now working overtime as I know JJ is involved, but I can't get a hold of him again. "Is he dead?" my thoughts started to go to a terrible place! I need to call Joe. Immediately I dial my husband's number, but the phone went to voicemail. I picked up the handset to call radio dispatch. "Emergency 265 this is Emergency 165 direct, go to white channel" I stated. "Emergency 165 this is Emergency 265, copy your traffic switching to white channel". I switched to white channel and shouted: "It's JJ you need to hurry up." "I'm clear," responds Emergency 265.

The longer this is taking to get to the scene, the more agitated I am becoming. I feel like Zach isn't driving fast enough. We arrive near the scene trying to figure out how to get back to JJ. The 911 dispatcher told us that there was a bonfire on the back part of the property and the vehicle was close to that spot. So as we are looking for the fire, I noticed some flames from a fire but how the heck do we get back there? Zach turned down a dirt driveway, but there was a creek separating us from the fire. "This is not right, Zach, we have to turn around!" I insisted, wanting to take the dang wheel! We pulled into the right driveway, and I could still see the fire, but again we didn't know how to get to it. At this point, I am desperately demanding Zach drive the ambulance through the field and get me to my son.

He quickly turned into the field and pressed the gas pedal to the floor to make sure we didn't get stuck. I remember seeing the glare of the fire, a spotlight, and a black jeep. On the radio dispatch call, it stated that there was a jeep rollover but this jeep didn't look wrecked or damaged. I could see two individuals by the black jeep, and one was lying motionless, and the other was over the top of him doing what looked like chest compressions. I couldn't make out the faces. Emergency 265 arrived at the crash site slightly before we did and I could see the medic running towards the scene with his medic bag and equipment. My driver drove up to the fence and put the ambulance in park, and I jumped out and went running, forgetting my medic bag and equipment. I got to the fence where a man was holding the wires up for me to run through and I screamed: "are these wires live"? The man replied "No", and I ran right through them. As I was racing up to the scene, I could see JJ. He was covered in blood dripping off his face, his hands were behind his head, and he was getting up from beside this motionless body and walking towards the back of the jeep. I felt so relieved that even though JJ was covered in blood, he was alive.

As I approached the motionless body, my initial relief quickly turned to panic as I discovered that it was Casey, JJ's best friend. Not only JJ's best friend, but a second son to my husband and I. Quickly, I squatted down near Casey's head, looking over his motionless body, trying to figure out what happened. I kept looking at JJ and asking him if he was ok and he kept screaming at me to worry about Casey not him, he is fine. As I was working to save Casey's life, I remember speaking to Casey as if he could hear me. "Casey, don't you leave us, this isn't your day to die," I said. "Casey come on now, you need to breathe, you need to breathe! Casey don't you dare die on me!"

The more his motionless body lay there unresponsive, the more I started to panic. I was thankful when I saw Samaritan Life Flight landing as I knew we needed their help to save Casey's life. As the crew from Samaritan got up to Casey, I gave a run-down of what I knew, which wasn't much, and one of the medics looked at me and said, "We got this, go be a mom". I walked over to JJ and put my arms around his neck, and we both just started crying. JJ kept hitting the back of his head on the tire of the jeep and kept saying, "I'm so sorry, Casey, I'm so sorry."

A few minutes later, Casey Sanders was pronounced dead, and JJ and I completely lost it.

As Samaritan life-flight took off and went back to the hospital without a patient, a police officer approached JJ and said: "Son, are you ok?" JJ stated, "yes, sir." "Have you been drinking son?" the officer asked, and JJ replied, "yes, we all were." The officer asked JJ a few more questions and then said he would be back.

After the officer left, I looked at JJ and asked: "how much did you have to drink JJ"? JJ shot back "a few". I looked him in the eye and said, "if you are drunk you will be responsible for Casey's death." He simply said, "I know mom, I know." I hugged JJ and put my forehead to his and said: "you know I love you, right buddy." "Yea mom, I know" was his response.

As I was sitting there with my son, I could see Joe heading up the field. I immediately started crying. I knew that this was going to break Joes' heart. As Joe approached us, JJ stood up, and Joe grabbed him and hugged him for what seemed like forever. Joe asked JJ if he was ok, and all I heard JJ say was "Casey's dead because of me." Joe was crying and was still hugging JJ, and Joe said: "JJ, we will get through this." JJ just cried harder.

The police officer came back over to us and explained to JJ that since he was drinking, he needed to have a blood alcohol test to determine if he was legally drunk. JJ stated ok, and he stood up and started walking with the officer. As JJ and the officer got to the police car, the officer handcuffed JJ and put him in the police car. Joe and I stood there in shock as our only son, who had just graduated from technical college, was being handcuffed and taken away in a police car.

As we were leaving, Joe and I walked by the jeep, there was a white sheet over Casey, his body was still lying there on the ground motionless. I stopped for a second, and Joe hugged me, and he started crying. He said, "we'll get through this, Monica." We continued to the truck, and one of the firefighters came up to me and just hugged me and said: "I'm so sorry, Monica, I am so sorry." We got to the truck, and I let Joe know that we needed to call our attorney and get some advice about what to do next.

One of our good friends is an attorney, interestingly enough, also named

Casey. I called his cell phone at 3:30 am, and he answered. What a relief to have him answer. He advised us that there was a lawyer in his firm that handled these kinds of cases and he could provide guidance as to what we should do. He asked us to give him a few minutes, and he would have him call us.

As we were driving to the hospital, I was still trying to process what had just happened. My heart was breaking for Casey's mom, I wasn't sure if she had received the news yet. I kept trying to put myself in her shoes, and my heart just kept breaking.

After we arrived at the hospital, a doctor and nurse came into the room and suggested that since JJ was involved in an accident where someone had died, it would be a good idea to have him seen by a physician to make sure he didn't sustain any injuries. As a medic, I knew that his adrenaline would soon wear off and he was going to start feeling the pain if he was hurt, so JJ agreed to allow the doctor to do a cat scan. As JJ sat in the bed waiting to be taken down to the CT scanner, Joe was on the phone with our attorney, and he was relaying information from our attorney to JJ. Our attorney informed us that JJ could refuse a blood draw and his license would automatically be suspended, or he could consent to the blood draw and we would just pray that his blood alcohol level would read below the legal limits. Our attorney stated that if JJ's blood alcohol level is above a 0.15 that he would probably be charged with vehicular manslaughter. When we heard the words vehicular manslaughter, we started to freak out. We knew that this was JJ's decision, but we also knew that this could mean years in prison.

While having this conversation with the attorney, the police officer came in and said: "Will you consent to a blood draw"? I spoke up and said, "he and Joe are talking with an attorney, and he will let you know in a few minutes." The officer looked at me and stated: "Your son doesn't have the right to an attorney at this point." I stopped what I was doing and said: "wait a minute; JJ always has a right to an attorney." The officer told us he would call his supervisor and left the room. As the officer was leaving, JJ hit his breaking point and shouted after the officer: "Get a warrant." Joe and I looked at each other and knew that JJ had reached a point where his frustration was getting to him. He looked at us and just broke down again, crying hysterically and kept repeating "I'm so sorry Casey, I'm so sorry" as he covered his face with his hands.

The CT technician came for JJ and wheeled him down to CT. This gave Joe and I an opportunity to talk with the attorney without JJ present. Our attorney clearly informed us that this isn't good. No matter how you look at this, JJ is in a hard spot right now. The legal ramifications hadn't completely hit Joe and I just yet, we were simply going through the motions of trying to help JJ.

Joe started crying, which made me start crying again, and we just stood there and hugged. JJ's nurse came in and let us know she empathized with all of the pain we were experiencing, and she couldn't even imagine how JJ was feeling. She wanted to warn us that situations like these can make a person contemplate suicide. She asked if we had guns in the house, which we answered in the affirmative. She then politely let us know that it might be wise to lock them up or get them completely out of the house for the time being. We both thanked her for her kind words. As she left the room, I looked at Joe and said she's right. We can't allow JJ to get close to any guns with his mind and emotions in their current state.

JJ was wheeled back into his room, and you could tell he had been crying. I walked over to him and put my forehead to his forehead again and said: "you know I love you right." He said, "Yes, mom, I love you too."

A few minutes later, the police officer walked back into the room with a warrant for a blood draw from JJ. The officer looked at JJ and asked if he would cooperate with the warrant, and JJ said yes. The police officer read a statement to JJ, and then a lab technician came into the room. She asked JJ a few questions and got everything set up to take JJ's blood. As she was grabbing one of the vials, it almost fell on the floor, but JJ caught it for her. She kind of laughed and said, "you have good reflexes." She took JJ's blood and gave all the info to the officer. The officer stood by the sink filling out paperwork, and the doctor walked in and said that CT scan came back and everything looks good. She told JJ that he was very lucky and that she was very sorry to hear about his best friend.

The police officer turned to JJ and announced: "You are free to go." I stood there in confusion as I was under the impression that we would know what his blood alcohol was that night. The officer explained that since there is a death that the blood sample is sent to Indianapolis to be tested, and it could be months before we get the results.

After finally making it home, and with JJ upstairs sleeping, I grabbed a cup of coffee and went into the living room, sat down on my favorite chair and put my legs up on the ottoman. As I sat there, I glanced down at my pants. There was dried blood on my knees. I completely broke down. For the first time, I was able to slow down and start to fully take in the calamity that had just rocked our family and community.

I lost all sense of time, and it would take days for the story to unfold. It was a rollercoaster of emotion from deep sadness for Casey and his parents and siblings, to fear for my son and his future and his mental health. As details of the events of that night began to unravel, the whole tragedy became more and more complicated with so many actors and so many lives forever changed.

The day after the accident, many of JJ and Casey's mutual friends made a steady stream to our house. They were crying, expressing condolences and comforting each other with memories of Casey. As they talked, details about that party became clearer. JJ and Casey both attended a graduation party/bonfire in the backyard of the graduates house, a common way to celebrate in the Midwest. There was plenty of alcohol provided at the party, we would later learn provided by one of the parents of the graduate. JJ and Casey left the party in separate vehicles and came back to our house. Casey then discovered that he had left his cell phone at the bonfire and wanted to return to retrieve it. JJ knew that Casey was in no condition to drive, and since he felt okay to drive, told Casey to jump in the jeep. They went back to the party, Casey got his phone and as they were leaving someone yelled out "Do a donut!". Casey was hanging out of the passenger side, sitting on the window sill, unrestrained, and JJ proceeded to do a donut in the field, barely going 30 miles an hour when JJ heard something "snap" and the jeep rolled on its side, pinning Casey under the roll bar. JJ was trying to get his seatbelt off, when he realized the jeep was on top of Casey, he began to yell out for help. As some of the teens raced over to try to put the jeep back upright, one of the girl's called 911. She was answering the 911 operators questions while they uprighted the jeep, and then she was disconnected. She began running away, and the rest of the teens followed her lead and ran from the scene, leaving in their vehicles. JJ was left alone with Casey, unresponsive on the ground. JJ called 911. When the operator asked what was the emergency, JJ responded, "We were being dumb asses and flipped the jeep, and a guy got pinned." The 911 operator then inquired about who was injured and there was silence. JJ never came back to the phone.

JJ knew that he could never run away and just leave Casey, he continued to do everything he could to save his life until help arrived. He and Casey had a motto, "Never leave a brother behind". He failed to understand how all of the others would just run away. This fact explained all of the traffic on the road heading away from the accident as we arrived in the ambulance.

The next weeks and months became a blur. It was a horrible rollercoaster of emotion. From the grief of Casey's funeral and saying good-bye, to the detectives and prosecutor and legal issues, to having a husband who is the Mayor of our small town and being in the spotlight as "The Baby Box Lady" and having a microscope being placed on our personal lives. It was all too overwhelming. I knew that my priority had to be my son, walking beside him and helping him get through this tragedy. I couldn't do the work for him, but I was determined to not let him walk this journey alone. Joe and I would be behind him every step of the way.

On July 1st, 2016, JJ was officially charged with two felonies and a misdemeanor. I asked our attorney to explain the charges and he stated that JJ's blood alcohol was .085 so he was charged with OWI—causing death, OWI—causing death with at least a BAC of 0.80 and underage consumption. At first I felt relief that the charge was not vehicular homicide, but quickly realized the seriousness of the charges JJ was facing. As we were leaving our attorney's office, having bonded JJ out, Joe said something to JJ that brought me to tears. I remember his words like he spoke them yesterday:

"JJ, you know how much we love you, right"? JJ responded, "yes." Joe continued, "I want you to know that I am very upset with your actions that night before the jeep tipped, but I couldn't be prouder of your actions after that jeep tipped, when you stayed behind and tried to save Casey." My eyes filled up with tears as JJ replied: "I know I let you down, and I'm sorry." Joe said, "We will get through this together, you know that your mom and I will always be a soft place for you to fall."

During the months of pretrial depositions, all of the evidence began to trickle in. The violation of the Indiana "Social Host Law" which holds adults liable that provide alcohol on their property for minor consumption responsible for the outcome, as well as a mechanical problem with the jeep itself. The pictures entered as evidence of the jeep revealed a broken spring on the passenger side rear tire of the jeep, clearly explaining why the jeep had tipped over. There was also evidence of mishandling of the case by detectives, who did not follow protocol. The only explanation I could comprehend was that they were prejudiced by my being an EMT on the scene, and knowing that JJ's father was the Mayor of Woodburn. Despite all of this evidence that pointed to the perfect storm of bad decisions fueled by alcohol and a busted spring on the jeep, JJ made the decision on his own to plead guilty. I was devastated, and very fearful of the outcome of his decision.

I will never forget the first words that JJ spoke to the Judge at his sentencing hearing. He had carefully written every word the night before, and with all of his family, his friends and Casey's family sitting in that courtroom, JJ began:

"I stand before you a broken man, A man that wishes every day I could go back to May 26 and make a different choice".

My heart broke, I was already in tears, there was grief for everyone in that room. There were no winners here. A family lost their youngest son, friends lost "the glue that had held them together" as they described Casey, and this mother and father were about to watch their only son be carted off to prison. Mixed with all of this grief and pain, I felt a sense of pride rising in me. I was so proud of my son, who right before my very eyes was becoming a man, a man of principle and courage. We had always taught him as a boy to take responsibility for his actions, to not run and hide or blame others. And here he was, facing unknown prison time, taking full responsibility for his part in the tragedy. While other adults and his peers distanced themselves and ran from their own actions that night, JJ openly owned the part he played in the devastation that occurred on May 26, 2016. In that moment I knew that JJ would come through this stronger, better and more empathetic to all around him. I was about to witness pain become purpose in the life of my own son.

JJ served 13 months in Indiana State Prison, the last 8 months on work release at the South Bend Re-entry Center, after leaving that facility he was placed on house arrest for one year. He was also required to complete community service, and probation for 2 years after release. During this time, a powerful documentary was produced and released titled "Never Leave A Brother Behind; JJ's Story". This documentary is being used in high school classrooms across the country as a potent reminder of the consequences of underage drinking. JJ also began to share his story in high schools across Indiana. I witnessed him making an impact on the lives of students every time he told his story. If it saves just one life from the tragedy we have been through, every second will be redeemed.

I have a tattoo on my left arm that signifies "the call that changed it all" May 26th, 2016. It's presence a constant reminder of that fateful day. I was temporarily sidelined from my mission with Safe Haven Baby Boxes, as walking with JJ required so much of my focus and attention. It also became difficult to continue in my work as an EMT and I would soon retire from the ambulance service. But on November 7th, 2017 everything changed again as my cell phone rang out in the middle of the night "We have a baby in the box!".

Chapter 9

EVERY LIFE HAS PURPOSE

"Get your fire back. It's not over until God says it's over. Start believing again. Start dreaming again. Start pursuing what God put in your heart."
author unknown

Sometimes the most monumental moments in your life happen when you are completely unprepared. This one was certainly no different. Teresa, my biological cousin, and I were boarding a plane to Arkansas to visit with family, with whom I had just been reunited in the past few years. We were excited for the trip ahead as we made our way to our seats in the back of the plane. When we landed, I noticed that I had quite a few missed calls from Warren Smith, the assistant chief firefighter at Coolspring Volunteer Fire Dept, home of Baby Box #2. He had left a few voicemails, but because it was pretty late at night, I decided to just call him without listening to his voicemails. When I finally got him on the phone, he just blurted out "We just got our FIRST BABY in the box!"

I could barely believe what I was hearing as Warren was excitedly describing to me what had just happened. The silent alarm was received around 10:25 pm and Chief Mick Pawlik and the other firefighters rushed to the station. On his way to the station, Mick told Warren not to bother coming, it was probably a false alarm and he would take care of it. Chief Mick was the first to arrive on scene in under 4 minutes from the time the alarm was triggered, still wearing his pajamas. He was still thinking it was just a prank, but as he approached the box, he saw what appeared to be a sweatshirt and a tiny baby's arm as he peered through the holes in the box's interior. Still thinking it must be a doll, he opened the box to retrieve it and the baby girl just stared right at him. He couldn't believe what he was seeing! This was a real live baby! The adrenaline set in and he had a hard time even talking on his portable radio, he blurted out "we have a baby in the cage!" I have no idea where the word "cage" came from, but that is what the media picked up from monitoring the 911 system.

Warren didn't listen to Mick when he suggested that he not come, and was on scene almost immediately. Chief Mick, pajamas and all, and Warren rode with the baby in the ambulance to the hospital. Chief kept saying "it's like we are proud Papa's!" barely able to contain his joy. I think he even admitted to me that he almost kissed Warren in the ambulance as they were so excited!

The baby girl was about one hour old and the umbilical cord was still attached. The hospital said she was in perfect condition, but would stay in the hospital for observation until the Department of Children's Services took custody.

It worked! All of those hours, months and years of hard work, legislation, fighting the state bureaucracy and all of the naysayers, were worth every second! A baby girl was safe, she was alive and her heroic mother had made the choice to keep her baby safe and give her a forever family, rather than abandon her to the elements.

Warren, Mick and the firefighters and paramedics with the Coolspring Volunteer Fire Department decided to name the baby girl "Hope". This was such a perfect name for the very first baby to be placed in a baby box in the United States. Hope represented the hope for this beautiful little baby's future. But not only hope for her, for every baby that would be rescued in these boxes, who without this option, might not survive.

Why did this happen when I had just arrived in Arkansas? Everything in me wanted to take the next flight out with Teresa so that we could both be with Warren and Mick and attend the press conference in person! The word was already out and my cell phone was ringing incessantly, so many media outlets were looking for details about the surrender. Neither Teresa and I got any sleep that night. Our hotline counselor, Pam Stenzel, was in Las Vegas at a church speaking with parents and teens. She wasn't answering her phone initially because she was on stage, the hotline continued to roll over to our back up. When she finished, she called me back to find out the news. We both couldn't believe the timing! She also got absolutely no sleep that night (and for a few days) answering the hundreds of hotline and media calls!

We decided that Mick and Warren could handle the press conference and I would continue to do interviews on Skype and talk to individual media outlets from Arkansas.

Some might wonder why it is important to do a press conference and let the public know about the baby surrendered in the box. There are many reasons, but chief among them is that we are sharply cognizant, having heard from mother's who surrendered their newborns, that these moms are scouring the news and internet for any word on the surrender. They desperately want to know that their baby is safe and in the hospital and will be cared for. Some have told us that they hung on every word we said at the press conference, which is a primary reason we are insistent on praising this brave mother for making the right decision and keeping her baby safe. This is a judgement free zone! I will not tolerate anyone making disparaging comments about this mother or her choice to surrender, not publicly or on any of our social media pages. She needs to be commended and encouraged. This also sends a message to any woman experiencing this crisis, that they have a last resort option and that they can and must keep their baby safe.

One of the other important reasons to have a press conference and let the public know about a safe, legal surrender, is that this is the prime opportunity for education. As I have shared earlier, just putting a box in a fire station or hospital, cannot by itself save a life. The community must know it exists and that they can legally choose to surrender by utilizing the box or by handing the baby to a firefighter, paramedic or hospital staff face to face. I wanted to make sure that the entire community was aware of the Safe Haven Law and legal ways to surrender a newborn, and that our 24 hour hotline received the coverage. If and when a young mother was facing this crisis, she would know to call the hotline or find us in a google search, and get the information she needed to make the best choice for her and her baby. You have to literally blanket the population with this knowledge, because you have no idea who needs that information and when.

That morning we released the following to the press:

For immediate release - November 8, 2017

18 Months after the installation of Safe Haven Baby Box #2 at the Coolspring Township Fire Department in Michigan City, a baby girl was successfully surrendered and turned over to the Indiana Department of Child Services late on November 7, 2017. The surrender took under 5 minutes, from the opening of the box to the arrival of First Responders taking possession of the child.

This brings the 2017 total of safe surrenders in Indiana to six, with zero illegal abandonments.

With the acrimony of the previous legislative session, Safe Haven Baby Boxes stood firm in their assertion that a viable option to abandonment needed to exist in Indiana. Webpages, email, and fliers may present the illusion of action, but it is the outreach and education that Safe Haven Baby Boxes provides that make the difference between a safe surrender and an illegal abandonment. Having the box available as an avenue for surrender presents a tangible way to prevent illegal abandonment in Indiana.

While anonymous surrender in the Baby Box is an option of last resort, this surrender serves to validate the existence of the Safe Haven Baby Box system and the procedures that ensure a safe, anonymous surrender.

Safe Haven Baby Boxes INC. is a Non-Profit organization 501(c)3.

Well, we succeeded in getting media coverage. That was an understatement! We were barraged with requests for interviews and the story went viral. I gave interviews to Chicago area television stations, print media and then Fox News, CNN, ABC New York and a full feature story on EWTN. We were even mentioned on Rush Limbaugh's Radio program! We were completely unprepared for the flood of hotline calls that followed. I believe we received thousands of calls that week. Have I mentioned that none of us were getting sleep!

Baby Hope, our very first Safe Haven Baby Box baby, was placed with her forever family just a few weeks after being surrendered. As soon as I returned from Arkansas, I made a b-line for Michigan City. I was so grateful that baby Hope's foster mother brought little Hope to the station and I was able to hold her in my arms. What a miracle she is! That day at the Coolspring Fire Station, baby Hope also had the opportunity to be hugged and snuggled by her proud "Papa's" and all who had a hand in saving her life. She truly continues to be a beacon of Hope for myself and everyone associated with Safe Haven Baby Boxes.

My passion was re-ignited, and the flame was burning hotter than it ever had before!

In April of 2018, we had a second surrender in the baby box in Coolspring Volunteer Fire Department. Once again, the thrill of seeing that little baby and pulling him out of the box was as exciting as rescuing baby Hope. He was beautiful, and perfect and we were so proud of mom for making the choice to keep him safe. Just days after the surrender we received a call from birthmom. As I talked with her, the conversations shed new light on the plight of these moms, on their mental state, and gave me deep insight into how much these precious babies are loved. In the box there is information available for the mother surrendering to take about her own physical health as well as information on how to contact us if they needed or wanted contact in the future. We also provide a registry on our website where a parent can, with complete anonymity, give important medical information, and a way they could be contacted if the adoptive family or child ever desired contact.

Since that first surrender in November of 2017, we have had 10 safe surrenders in our boxes to date. Ten beautiful babies who now have a forever family, a future and HOPE:

November 2017, Michigan City IN
April 2018, Michigan City IN
September 2019, Hammond, IN
December 2019, Crown Point, IN
January 2020, Seymour, IN
February 2020, New Haven, IN
May 2020, Benton, AR
June 2020, New Haven, IN
October 2020, Decatur Township, IN
November 2020 - Undisclosed, IN

As I look over this list, I see more than just a date and location. I see a beautiful life, a unique child who is loved by their creator and was given a plan and purpose. Jeremiah 29:11 states: "For I know the plans I have for you," declares the Lord, "plans to prosper you and not to harm you, plans to give you hope and a future."

In the middle of a cold winter night, our hotline coordinator was awakened by the sound of a fireman's pager, the ringtone she chose for the hotline that jolted her from sleep. Clearing her head, she listened to the mom on the other end who was wanting information about surrendering her newborn. The counselor explained the safe haven law, gave information about the box and it's operation, as well as information on how to find the nearest baby box to her. The counselor reminded her that she could place any information about her baby that she would want the medical personnel and adoptive family to have, in writing, with the baby when she surrendered. She encouraged this mom to call back if she needed any further assistance and encouraged her to get the medical and counseling help that she needed going forward. Within 24 hours of that call, a baby girl was surrendered in one of our boxes.

As the firefighters retrieved this infant from the baby box, they noticed a handwritten note placed in the blanket with the baby. They gave me a copy of the note, and as I held it in my hand and read the words, carefully and lovingly written by this mother, tears rolled down my face.

Dear Baby,

I just want you to know that
the short time I had with you
was so beautiful and every ounce
of love I have I gave you
the decision to give you to a
family was by far the hardest
I've ever made you are so
beautiful, sweet, little bundle
of pure joy.
If I had everything you needed
I would have absolutely kept
you but I don't have all of
the things you need it is the
right thing to do. I don't want
to cheat you out of a beautiful
life. I fear we would have had
a very hard time. thats not
fair to an innocent beautiful
baby. I will think of you every
day and I hope that someday
you notice and have an
intuition when you feel it in
your heart its me (cooking,
the smell of fresh linen
candles, dragon flies, a love for

Birth mom gave permission to print

animals, and a gentle side -
even if you are a firecracker)
♡

Remember I loved you so
much.. I would have called
you Mila. If and and when
you or your parents want
to know who I am. post
an ad on facebook North
West Indiana.

Medical info

No use of drugs or illicit
substances.
all Healthy siblings -
My Blood Type A+
No none health problems

you were breastfed for 1st
24 hrs - and had a small
amount of formula
you were born @ 3:04 am
December 4th,
1 bath -

*I will call the local hospital to check + answer questions

How can you read this and not feel the love mixed with incredible pain and loss. You have read with your own eyes the reason we call each of these mothers "hero's"! This is truly "brave love", to be able to put your self interest last and do what is best for your child. This is the polar opposite of the selfish act of illegal abandonment. This is truly a human model of the love Christ showed us when he gave his life on the cross as atonement for our sin.

We have kept in contact with this hero of ours, and she has such a passion to assist us with our mission, to help people understand what these mom's experience, as well as to help other women facing a similar crisis. I was so grateful that she was willing to write down her story and share it with our supporters at a fundraising event we held in August of 2020. We disguised her voice and kept her in shadows, but she was able to share her powerful message with us that evening. Here is that message:

On a cold night in 2019, after a 6 hour labor, I delivered a healthy baby girl alone at home by myself.

I kept her at home loving and snuggling her for 36 hours, struggling to make the right decision for her future. Selfishly I wanted to keep her, but I knew that there were better options for this sweet baby that I would have called Mila.

She deserved the world and so much more.

After hours of research and articles, I read about the Safe Haven Baby Boxes program. I could have gone to a hospital, police, or fire station, but being 100% anonymous was the only option for me.

There are questions you have to answer at those locations that could have put myself or my baby in danger. And anyone knowing my identity could be deadly for either of us.

After reading Monica's story and the choice her biological mother made and the strength she has now gave me the strength to make the biggest decision of my life and my baby's life.

I decided that the only option I could live with was utilizing the Safe Haven box.

There were no cameras or anyone I had to justify my decision to.

I also didn't want them talking me out of this decision. This decision was made entirely out of love for her.

I am truly grateful for this option being available in my community.

I can sleep at night knowing my baby is safe.

I eventually made the decision to reach out to Safe Haven Baby Boxes after I placed my baby in the baby box.

I have received updates from Monica. I never expected that.

I have received help with no judgement, and I feel at peace with my decision. As I work with Monica and her crew, I become emotionally stronger every day.

I left a two page letter with my baby when I placed her in the baby box and all of the items and the letter I left with her, were given to her forever family. If they choose to contact me that is an opportunity I would be so grateful for.

Please don't hesitate on this opportunity to save lives.

There are many mothers just like me who just need a little help to make the right decision. An option that offers no judgement or questions.

I could never say it better than this mother did. She clearly explained why we do what we do, why I have fought so hard to have this truly anonymous option available for women. I will be forever grateful for the heart of this young woman, for her compassion for others and her willingness to allow her pain to bring purpose and healing and save many lives in the future.

In January of 2020, a newborn was surrendered in our box in Seymour, Indiana. This surrender was special to us because of the hard work and resilience of a young man, now a college student, Hunter Wart. Hunter wanted to have a baby box in his community, he knew it was a big undertaking, but as a senior in high school, he dedicated his senior year project to raising the funds for a baby box. He raised money by selling scrap metal and mowing lawns, and was able to raise $10,000 to have this box installed at the fire station.

Hunter said he was glad his hard work had paid off. In an interview with a local media outlet, he said the following:

"I'm glad that the mother brought her baby safely to the baby box, and I want my hard work to pay off for a long time," Hunter said. "This is the first baby to have been surrendered to this box and she will now be known as Baby Mia."

Hunter told the media that usually the firefighters or Safe Haven Baby Boxes gets to name the baby, but since he worked so hard to donate this box to his community, we gave him the honor of giving this precious baby a name.

Baby Box #3 was installed in the Decatur Township Fire Station. The folks there worked so hard to bring this box to their community. I made the mistake (forgive me, we were new at this whole thing) of announcing the box location before it was ready to go "live" and wouldn't you know it, the fire station was held up by stupid paperwork. As a matter of fact, it was held up by a "flood permit"! You can't make this stuff up, a "flood permit" for installing a baby box in a FIRE STATION! It took a few weeks before the box was actually functional, but we had already announced its presence in the media.

It was a typical "duty day" and firefighter Bryan Mink was eating dinner with the rest of the crew. He finished his dinner first, he told me he was a fast eater because he is so picky. The phone rang and Brian picked it up. There was someone outside who wanted one of the firefighters to meet him at the door. Bryan didn't think much of it, and went to the front door to see who it was. He could see through the doorway, there was a man holding a basket. It is not unusual for people to come by the station and drop off food for the firefighters so Bryan's first thought was that it was a fruit basket. He stepped out and said "Thanks so much", and the man looked up at him with tears in his eyes. Brian was kind of taken back by the emotion, so he pulled back the blanket covering the basket, and looking at him was a tiny baby.

The man, in tears, told Bryan that he didn't want to have to do this but they had to do what was best for the baby and were surrendering under the safe haven law. Bryan didn't know this, but the mother was still in the car on the phone with our hotline counselor, who had given instructions on the law and the process. We also encourage them to leave a note, which they did, tucked inside the basket.

Bryan was still in shock, but walked back into the dining area where the rest of the firefighters were finishing dinner. He placed the basket on the table and pulled the blanket off. Their response was "Cool, whose baby is that?" Bryan said "This baby was just surrendered under the safe haven law." No one could believe it! They had never had a baby surrendered at their station before and now this happened just weeks before the box would have been available.

They took the baby by ambulance to the hospital where this little one was in NICU for a little over three weeks. During that time, Bryan and his wife were the only ones given permission to visit this precious baby until the adoptive parents could be gifted with him. Every day, either Bryan or his wife, if Bryan was on duty, came up to the NICU and held this little one and loved on him as he officially had no parents. There is a special bond between these firefighters with every baby that is surrendered, but this went above and beyond. It is an amazing bond that exists to this day, as Bryan and his wife get regular updates and have even attended family celebrations with this special little boy.

Just a few months ago, another baby was surrendered, this time in the working baby box at the Decatur Township Fire Station. As fate would have it, the first EMT firefighter on scene was Bryan Mink's son! His son had been an EMT for less than six months, and this moment will be with him for his entire career. We've decided that the Minks are pretty special, and that all of them will have to have an opportunity to be a part of the life-changing experience of a safe haven surrender.

As I retell the stories of these precious little ones, of their moms and dads, and of all those who had a part in each one being kept safe and being given a forever family, my heart is bursting. Each one of these children is made in the image of God. They are a unique creation with a specific plan and purpose for their life. Maybe one of these precious ones will take my place in about 20 years if God allows me to retire! In their eyes, we see hope for generations. We see the hand of God, redeeming and calling each one for His Glory. You cannot put a price tag on just one of the lives of these precious babies. Their existence reminds all of us that "we know that in all things God works for the good of those who love him, who have been called according to his purpose." Romans 8:28

Chapter 10

HERE AM I LORD, SEND ME

"Be the kind of woman that when your feet hit the floor each morning, the Devil says, 'Oh crap, she's up'"!

It's a cool morning in Lebanon, Indiana on November 7th of 2020. I am standing outside Lebanon Fire Station #11 with the firefighters, the Mayor, Linda Znachko, and around fifty people from the community, blessing Baby box #47. Linda gave us all a powerful reminder of the footprint of Baby Amelia, placed on the signage of every Baby Box, a testament to the fact that her life mattered and that she left her footprint as "defender" of the lives of each and everyone of these babies saved from abandonment. My heart was moved again, as it is on every occasion I get the chance to hear Linda speak so passionately about the honor and dignity she and her organization have given to so many abandoned infants.

After Linda finished speaking, I introduced Pastor Ben and invited him to come up and say a few words, to pray a blessing over our 47th Baby Box in America. As Pastor Ben began sharing, my heart was pierced with his words. It was as if God was speaking directly to me, audibly, reminding me of His call on my life, not just in South Africa, but that call that was spoken over me from the moment of my conception.

Pastor Ben began with the story of Isaiah, a very old story that took place around 742 b.c. Isaiah heard the call of God on his life to speak to the people on His behalf, at a time when society was in a pretty dark place and they needed God's help. Isaiah 6:8 states "Then I heard the voice of the Lord saying, 'Whom shall I send? And who will go for us?' And I said, 'Here am I Lord. Send me!'" Pastor Ben continued to remind us that we were in Lebanon today because I had heard those words years ago and also answered, "Here am I Lord, send me!" My soul said "Yes" and "Yes" again as I listened to Pastor Ben. Everything in me resonated with that scripture and that description of the call of God. I knew in that moment, that with such a great cloud of witnesses (Hebrews 12:1) who had come before me, I had indeed heard and heeded the call of God on my life.

Pastor Ben then read the words of the old hymn "Here I Am, Lord"

I, the Lord of sea and sky,
I have heard my people cry.
All who dwell in darkness now
My hand will save.
I who make the stars of night,
I will make their darkness bright.
Who will bear my light to them?
Whom shall I send?
Here I am, Lord. It is I Lord.
I have heard you calling in the night.
I will go, Lord, where you lead me.
I will hold your people in my heart.

What a powerful way to dedicate this box, and such an amazing witness to me personally, of the call and purpose for my life. What a journey this has been, and it isn't finished yet! The call of God can often feel overwhelming, and answering it with "Here am I" almost always brings strong feelings of inadequacy. How could the Creator of the universe call me, a seemingly insignificant, unqualified woman who had such a conspicuous beginning. But the truth is, He did call me. The old saying that "God doesn't call the qualified, He qualifies the called" is certainly true. We need only to say "Yes" and remain faithful to Him. It is truly my heart's only desire to one day run into the arms of my Savior and hear him say "Well done, Thou good and

FAITHFUL servant".

Yes, there is more race to be run, but I am so thankful for the hand of God each and every mile. As I write this, we now have 54 baby boxes in 4 states. We have assisted with 97 safe surrenders of infants across the country, 10 of these surrendered in one of our boxes. We have taken over 8,000 hotline calls and helped countless women with an adoption or parenting plan. We have walked alongside mothers who have surrendered, offering counseling, material assistance and even legal help for a few who were in need.

I will never forget this particular story. In the middle of the night, the hotline rang once again. The voice of the mother on the other end of the line was calm and measured. In fact, our hotline counselor was amazed at how calm and assured this mom was as she reached out for help. She had delivered her baby at home, alone, as so many of our mothers do, which is astounding in and of itself. She called wanting to know the closest baby box so that she could truly surrender anonymously. When we realized the closest box was over 50 miles away, we began to explore every other option for her. She was determined to surrender, but was adamant that she did not want a face to face surrender. We suggested she call 911 and have the paramedics come to her. She didn't want them showing up at her house, so she made a decision to drive to a Walmart, and call 911 from there. She did exactly that in the wee hours of the morning and when the ambulance arrived, she placed the baby in the paramedics arms and told him she was surrendering under the safe haven law.

I received the call about the surrender from the hospital that received the infant asking about the protocols for a safe haven surrender, this was obviously the first time they had encountered this! I headed to the fire station later in the day to speak with the firefighters who had received the baby. One of them admitted to me that, in fact, he knew this woman and I stressed to him what he already knew, but I still felt the need to make sure that he absolutely must keep her identity confidential. This fire station now has a baby box of their own, so that women in these rural areas will also have an option of a complete anonymous surrender.

This story illustrates again, how important the Baby Box program is and why so many of these mothers seek complete anonymity. While the safe haven laws, available in all fifty states, provide "confidentiality", they certainly do not provide complete anonymity.

One of the greatest blessings I have experienced as I have pursued my mission and God's call, is to partner with so many amazing people who have come alongside me in this journey. None of us travels our path alone. God is so gracious to provide us with partners who share our passion. I could fill pages with all of the people who have had an impact on Safe Haven Baby Boxes. From Linda Znachko, and our common passion for abandoned infants, to Casey Cox and the many legislators in Indiana and so many other states across the country who have joined us in passing laws to protect babies and provide mothers with a safe, legal, anonymous last resort option.

I think of my board members as well as my small staff and volunteers. And while they may complain about me being "their boss", they never fail to step up when they are called upon to get the work done. Kevin Albin has faithfully kept up with our social media presence, answered questions, he helps with "Beyond The Box" and all of our Facebook Live events. Priscilla Pruitt and her husband Sean have supported our mission almost from the beginning. Priscilla has contributed so much to our awareness and education campaign as well as translating our signage and information into Spanish.

I can't forget my good friend Cathie Humbarger, from Allen County Right to Life. She has been an encourager, she has allowed me to pick her brain for ideas for legislation, lobbying and development. She represents the community of pro life advocates who have supported our efforts across the country in so many ways.

My early partnership with the Knights of Columbus and all of the amazing men who make up this incredible organization, and their wives as well, have been a true blessing. I am not sure how far we would have come if they had not believed in the mission from the very beginning, and fought with me through all the obstacles thrown my way. I am particularly grateful to Scott, the former Grand Knight for the state of Indiana. His commitment to us and the mission of Safe Haven Baby Boxes did not waver.

I must mention all of the amazing firefighters, paramedics and first responders who have fought so hard to have a baby box available in their communities. Warren Smith, from Coolspring Volunteer Fire Department was one of the first to believe in my mission without wavering. He received so much push back from the Department of Children's Services and other officials, but he never caved in or gave up on having an active baby box in his station. These first responders have lobbied city councils, raised money and raised awareness in their communities. I have spent time in their fire stations and hospitals, training on the safe haven law and legal surrender of newborns. We have truly developed a special bond and it feels so good to walk into these stations across the country and just feel right at home again in their presence.

I think of my dear friend, Corie Walls, and her precious daughter Ataya. Ataya was a huge supporter of Safe Haven Baby Boxes, attending events and fundraisers with her mom who volunteered her time with us. Tragically, Ataya, at age 14, was killed in a car accident in 2018. Ataya was a freshman at Leo Jr/Sr High School in Leo, Indiana at the time of her death. She carried a 4.0 GPA and was enrolling in college classes online, education was a top priority for Ataya. In memory of this beautiful young lady, taken from us way too soon, we have set up the Ataya Kaser Memorial Scholarship Fund. Money given to this fund will go directly to scholarship winners determined by our committee, to be used for their education. Every year, Safe Haven Baby Boxes will put out information about qualifying for this scholarship. We want to honor the life of Ataya by helping others achieve their education dreams. You can find out more info on this scholarship fund on our website.

And of course, I need to mention my dear family as I think of those who have impacted my journey. My parents, who have loved me unconditionally and instilled in me a deep sense of worth and love. It was their love and support that truly brought me through the difficult moments of finding purpose through pain. My siblings and nieces and nephews, whose support and love have meant so much as well. And of course, my children who have put up with my craziness, my time away, the crazy hours I have spent traversing the state and country. They have endured much without complaint (mostly) and have become true partners in this mission. And Teresa, my biological cousin, who continues to fight alongside me to ensure no woman makes the same mistake her aunt (my birthmom) did so many years ago. And most of all, my husband, Joe. There aren't enough words to describe the big part he has played in this entire journey. He has a true servant's heart, and is willing to do whatever is needed, never wanting the spotlight. He is truly my rock, my better half! I always remind everyone "I married up!"

I will be forever grateful for the mom's who have allowed me to be a part of their stories. They have shared their pain and grief, but mostly have given me deep insight to their incredible love for their babies. Each and everyone of them has left an indelible stamp on my life. And a big hug to the precious babies, whom I have had the privilege of holding, and snuggling and chasing! Just ask anyone who attended our Gala in August of 2020, I thought Baby Hope was going to run right off the platform in front of everyone! These babies are a constant reminder of the immense love the Father has for all us. I will also be forever grateful to the adoptive families who have welcomed us into their homes and hearts and have provided so much encouragement and support to me and the whole Safe Haven community. Their willingness to share their children and their story is an inspiration to so many. Adoption truly does unleash possibility!

As I look to the future in front of me, I am filled with anticipation. I have watched God do so much in such a short time, and I firmly believe that this is only the beginning. We are prepared to launch the baby box program in multiple states this coming year. The first being kicked off with the state of Florida! We are so excited to welcome Florida to the party in 2021. We firmly believe that we will be operating nationwide by 2025! Obviously this effort takes time, talent and treasure. You can partner with us in our mission by following us on social media, placing your email on our mailing list so you can keep updated on our progress. You will find more information on how to be involved, how to bring a baby box to your community and how to make a donation to our nonprofit on the website www.shbb.org or on the website accompanying this book. I hope you will take the time to go to this book's website, there is so much more available for you to learn and experience! And I sincerely hope that if my story has touched your life you will let me know! I can't wait to hear from you! And please, share this book with a friend, a family member, a neighbor. It takes all of us to make a difference in our communities, to be a light for the most vulnerable among us.

As I end this book, I have some parting thoughts I would like to leave with you. I am honored that you would come with me on this journey of self reflection. I have poured out my heart and life in these pages, not just as a catharsis for me personally, but more importantly to give glory to God and to acknowledge His hand on my life. I also desire that this book and my story would be an encouragement to each and every one of you. My journey is not unique in the sense that God has a plan for every one of us. A unique purpose to which He calls us all. I sincerely pray that when you hear His voice calling to you, asking "Whom shall I send", that your heart will cry out "Here am I, Lord, Send me!"

May God give you a sense of what He is up to in your life. May you see glimpses of the breakthrough that is just up ahead. May you, with all your heart, believe that trusting Him over what your eyes see, is totally and completely worth it. I pray that you will shift your weight off of your logical reasoning and onto the weightiness of His powerful promises to you. You have help and resources that go far beyond anything you could ever need. Smile with joy and walk by faith today. He has got you, He will never abandon you!

It is my prayer, as I trust it is yours, that when we reach the end of our journey here on earth, we will run into the embrace of Jesus! Oh, how I long for that moment, and how I pray I will hear the words "Well done, my good and faithful servant!"

Monica's parents   Married June 27, 1970

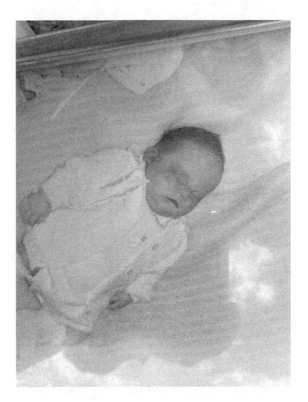

God's Garden

God's garden has need of a little
flower.
It had grown for a time here below,
But in tender love He took
it above.
In more favorable clime to grow.

"Suffer little Children to come unto Me
—for of such is the kingdom of God."

St. Luke 18:16

In Memory Of
ROBERT LEE SHAFFER JR.

Date Of Birth
JUNE 2, 1971

Date Of Death
JUNE 3, 1971

Place And Time Of Services
Taylor Funeral Home - Oakwood, Ohio
June 5, 1971 at 2:00 P. M.

CLERGYMAN
Reverend Richard Crosby

MUSIC
Kathryn Guyton

CASKET BEARERS
Roger Shaffer - Carl Sherry

PLACE OF INTERMENT
Melrose Cemetery

ARRANGEMENTS BY
Taylor Funeral Home - Oakwood, Ohio

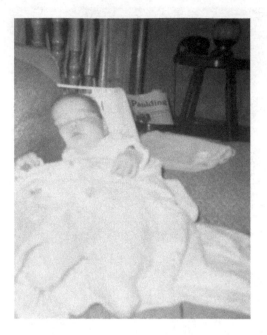

The day Monica was placed with her loving parents!

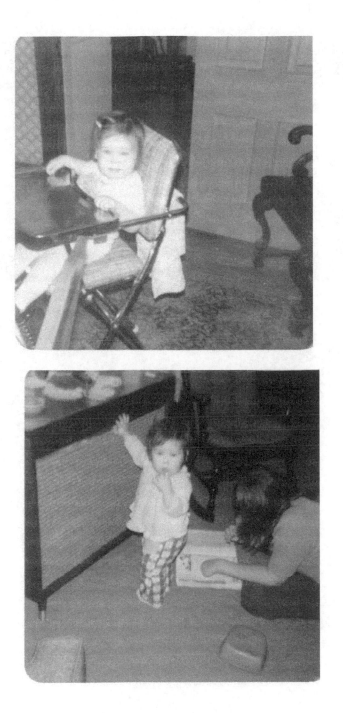

Saving Babies One Box At A Time

Parasailing in South Africa!

Dec 2013

Cape Town South Africa, Dec 2013

Signing of HB 1016 in 2015

Monica helping to make the 1st cut for Safe Haven Baby Box installation #1

Monica and Teresa

Proud Papa's from Coolspring Volunteer Fire Station

Monica and Linda Znackho honoring Baby Amelia.

Babies Saved with the help of Safe Haven Baby Boxes

Pricilla Pruitt, Mrs. International 2016

Safe Haven Baby Boxes National Spokesperson

Monica with an abandoned baby in Japan.

Monica with Pastor Lee from "The Drop Box"

Japan Baby Box Convention April 2018

Monica with her Dad.

Baby Saved by Safe Haven Baby Boxes

Ataya Kaser
Memorial Scholarship

Monica and her Birth mom Sandy

CPSIA information can be obtained
at www.ICGtesting.com
Printed in the USA
BVHW030451110722
641514BV00005B/22